MIRROR, MIRROR

Mirror, Mirror

confessions of a plastic-surgery addict

Terry Prone

SITRIC BOOKS

First published 2001 by
SITRIC BOOKS LTD
62–63 Sitric Road, Arbour Hill,
Dublin 7, Ireland

A CIP record for this title is available from
The British Library.

1 3 5 7 9 10 8 6 4 2

ISBN 1 903305 05 5

Chapter 2, 'Butterfly Christmas', first appeared in
Blood Brothers, Soul Sisters, a collection of short stories published
by Poolbeg in 1994; part of chapter 7 appeared in slightly different
form in the Sunday Independent.

Set in Georgia
Printed in Ireland by ColourBooks, Baldoyle, Dublin

CONTENTS

INTRODUCTION

If you want to know my verdict on an operation and how much I paid for it, look out for the boxes scattered throughout the text.

If you want to know the gory details of procedures, concentrate on Chapters 3, 5, 6, 8, 9, 10, 11 and 12.

If you want to learn more about ageism, the plastic/cosmetic/aesthetic surgery phenomenon, fitting it into a relatively normal life, and the fun I've had with it, read the rest.

MIRROR, MIRROR

1

A contradiction,
on the face of it

The chances are that you picked up this book for one of two reasons.

The Maybe reason.

Or the Shock, Horror, reason.

The Maybe reason goes like this:

"Maybe, at some point later in my life, I might just *possibly* consider some kind of plastic surgery, so I'd like to know how it works and what it costs."

If that's your reason, this is your book. It's written by someone who has experienced dozens of different kinds of plastic surgery at the hands of surgeons on both side of the Atlantic and who tells the truth about each procedure. Discomforts, results, costs and all.

The Shock, Horror reaction is where you go:

"Hey, I'm in the bookshop anyway, so let me just have a peep at this latest vapid outpouring by a shallow old bag who's trying to fight the natural ageing process. Just to confirm to myself that

I'd never sink to destroying the real character in my face, the real lines I've earned in life ..."

If that's your thinking, the book is for you too. Because – oddly enough – I'm with you. I'm not the type to have a face-lift. I have a great career, not dependent at all on my looks. Which is just as well, since my weight has gone from 10 stone to 16 stone and back for thirty years, erring on the side of 16 stone. My work involves me with people who concentrate on ideas, policies, corporate problems and staff development. My social life is non-existent, because when the day job is over, I eat, read books and write novels – therefore no partying or being looked at by others.

Yet I've had two face-lifts, a brow-lift and an arm-lift.

My complexion has been smoothed by laser resurfacing, my stomach flattened by liposuction, forehead wrinkles ironed out by injections of a potentially fatal bug. I've had a tummy-tuck, implants put in and taken out, make-up tattooed on and thready veins lasered off.

Over the past few years, summer holidays and long weekends have been devoted to this addiction. I've taken time off from work only for the dental and eye surgery – everything else has been done on my own time with nobody other than my husband knowing. Tom's attitude, now that you ask, is neutral-to-negative. In other words, he thinks I'm half mad and that there was nothing wrong with me to start with. But whatever turns me on ...

It has cost a lot of money. I could have had a swimming pool installed or be driving a Ferrari for what I have paid to cosmetic surgeons. (The dental implants alone cost £25,000.) Not all of it has worked, although only one bit of it left me worse off than I was beforehand.

If anyone had suggested to me, at thirty, that I would ever spend enormous amounts of money and time on plastic surgery, I would have laughed them to scorn. Plastic surgery was what ageing American actresses did – newspapers every now and then ran before-and-after shots of people like Faye Dunaway, the one on the left-hand side wrinkly, the one on the right smooth, and the caption doing a wink-wink job of telling readers that a scalpel or two had been at work here. Or plastic surgery was bought by American debutantes with over-arching noses and financially secure doting fathers. The entire plastic surgery phenomenon belonged within groups where youth and beauty are valued more than intellect or wisdom.

And then I had the car crash.

As car crashes go, it was the best kind to have. Spectacular – but nobody died and I have no memory of it. I'm told that I was driving to Galway on the last day of August, early on a wet afternoon, with the other side of the road filled bumper-to-bumper with returning holiday-makers. My small yellow Mazda came around a bend in the road near Lucan and there was another car, on my side of the road, facing me. Making progress, too: both of us seem to have been doing fifty miles an hour. Which meant that when we connected, his bigger, heavier estate car made £180 worth of scrap metal out of my new Mazda and pretty close to the same scrappage out of me.

The steering wheel caved in my cheekbones, broke my jaws, smashed my teeth. The seatbelt snapped across my throat and did away with my singing voice. The dashboard came across my left arm, breaking it in more than one place. The engine reversed all over my legs, reducing them to what a surgeon described as "eggshells in a polythene bag". My lung collapsed. My brain swelled.

The next weeks were filled with Intensive Care, operating theatres, confusion, pain and complications. When I demanded to go home – three months before it was medically advised – Tom took me home. Cared for me. Washed me. Lifted me. Fed me. Coped with my aphasia. (That's a form of brain damage. Amnesia for words.)

At that point, I had no idea that my appearance had been changed. Later, I published a short story about how I found out that it had. That's the next chapter. The "he" is my husband, Tom Savage. The "she" is me. Or what was left of me after the crash.

2

Butterfly Christmas

He had marched the Christmas trees out to where she sat in the car. Two by two, thumping their stumps into the pavement and twirling them. The first two she rejected.

"Spacer," she said decidedly, then shook her head as a wet dog does, two rigid hands rising off her lap to sketch in the air.

"Spacer," she said again, helplessly.

A couple of passers-by, one clutching two turkeys by the neck in much the same way as her husband was holding the trees, stopped to watch.

"Bigger around?" her husband asked.

She was silent.

"Taller?"

The nod was frantic.

"No problem," he said, and marched the shorter trees away.

The chosen tree was now anchored in a clever red contrivance that held water, and five sets of tiny lights had been threaded all over it. Today, he would put up the decorations. She went to turn in the bed and failed. The reflexes of mobility don't give up easily, she reflected. Nor the dreams filled with unplanned, unquestioned movement.

"Very fortunate your ribs weren't broken," he said, sliding out of his side of the bed and heading for the bathroom. "You'd never have managed without the deep sighs."

Snorting laughter overcame her, alone in the big bed. The snorts had been there since childhood, but in self-conscious adolescence she had developed the habit of cupping a hand over mouth and nose so that her laughter made a drowned noise.

Now, neither hand could reach mouth and nose. Thinking about this provoked an itch beside her nostril. She concentrated on it, having been taught that if you tried to make it get worse rather than better, you could eventually make it go away. Your brain lost interest in paying so much attention to one small irritant.

The itch stayed and worsened, unaware of the sophisticated psychology being applied to it. It took ownership of her as pain never had. In the intensive care unit, staff had driven her berserk by their solicitude for the pain. Pain control was now in fashion. Everybody was geared to stop it before it started, as opposed to the old days when it was allowed to become a raging torrent before the easing needle was employed. Nobody, however, was geared to take an itch seriously. And for her, the itches were worse than the pain.

He was beside her with a rough dry face-cloth. He rubbed it impersonally all over her face, scouring the itch away. The cloth then went into the bowl of hot water he had carried in, its coarse terry loops softening so that when he washed her face it was a warm wet infusion of comfort.

"This is gonna hurt you more than it hurts me," he said, as he now always did, before cleaning her teeth.

The jaws were locked, leaving only an inch of access. The brush, scrubbing against the enamel, was loud in her ears as he talked to her, the words lost. She looked a question at him, but he seemed contented with her lack of response, and dressed her, buttoning her shirt right up to the collar as if readying her in a school uniform.

"I've solved the problem of getting you downstairs," he said, as he looped one of her arms over his shoulders and lifted her.

As he carried her across the small landing, she could feel the redness rising in her face for shame at her own heaviness.

"Now I'm going to lean you against the wall and slide you down," he said, ignoring her anxious grunts.

The painted wall was smooth and chill against her white shirt as he slid her down to a sitting position at the top of the stairs where he had laid the duvet from the single bed. Once she was seated, he pulled the plaster rigidities of her legs out in front of her, pointing down the stairs towards where he was, a few steps below her. He tipped her forward so that her head was on his shoulder, and gently pulled the duvet, so that her bottom went bump from one stop to another, her forehead hitting the soft padded shoulder of his cardigan in an off-tempo echo. She began to laugh at the awkward efficiency of it, sucking in hairs from the cardigan at every in-breath.

Three steps from the bottom he straightened her up as briskly as if she had been a shop-mannequin, and hefted her into the wheelchair.

"*Now*," he said, kicking off the brake of the wheelchair with enormous satisfaction. "Now."

He parked her where she could watch the flames of the freshly-lit fire and went off to the other end of the long oblong room to start making breakfast. She could follow what he was doing by the sounds. Paper rustling and then a clunk as sliced bread was slid into a toaster.

A fainter click as the kettle went on. Cracking of eggshells and the chatty monologue of an egg frying. He always fried eggs too quickly so they developed a lacework of bubbles and a black edge.

"Oh, d'you know what ..." he said, coming over to the stereo and rifling through CDs. "What would you like?"

"Diminished fifth," she said. Quite clearly. He looked at her in intense silence, a CD in one hand, a tea-towel flung over his shoulder.

"Minor Detail?" he suggested. She nodded, wondering again at the scrambled brain that could so transpose a band's name. He sorted through carefully preserved old vinyls to come up with the LP, put it on, and went back to cooking, swearing to himself as the fat spat at him.

He had developed a way of feeding the two of them, mouthful about, which ensured both got hot food, but which required concentration on both parts. He got momentarily touchy when she turned her head away from a proffered bite of toast.

She was looking beyond him at the window of the converted eighteenth-century millhouse.

"Butterflies," she said. The word was muffled but unmistakable. Her husband sat back in his chair and went through his usual routine.

"Butter? No. Marmalade? Birds? Decorations? Music?"

"Butterflies," she said again, more firmly.

"Jesus, I can't figure," he said, baffled.

She butted her head in the direction she wanted him to look, but he was back with the problem of food.

"I'll work it out in a minute, OK?" he said, and inserted toast in her mouth as if he was a postman delivering a letter. For a moment, she considered shoving it back out with her tongue, but sucked it instead. The next time he arrived with a forkful of black lacy egg, she turned her head as far away as she could.

"OK," he said, ostentatiously patient. "OK. Butterflies."

He stood up, turned to the window, and a coloured cloud of them surrounded him. Some of them settled on him, the elaborate primary colours bright against the grey of his cardigan.

He stood in startled silence.

"Butterflies," he said again, his accent adding a soft aitch after the *t* so they became buttherflies. There were at least ten of them. He nudged the one on his shoulder and it shifted to the back of his hand. He brought it to her, placing it on the frame that held her wrist rigid.

For a few seconds, the russet and ultramarine wings fluttered anxiously, then were at peace. She watched for a long time in silence, rehearsing the words so they would come out right.

"At Christmas?"

The man nodded. "Never heard of that before. Maybe because it's thatched, the cottage. Maybe the eggs got laid and the warmth of the fire ..."

He poked the one on his arm until it flew off and settled on the Christmas tree, and then he put a fire-guard in front of the flames.

The room was warmer now and the butterflies flew high in the rafters as if in the branches of a tree in midsummer. She wanted to look more closely at the one on her wrist but could bring it no closer.

"Tantalus," she said aloud.

"Yeah," her husband said, picking up the plates and heading for the sink.

Not being able to get a proper view of the butterfly tainted the pleasure of it being there at all, she realized. It was like having eye-floaters, those oddly shaped images that stay constantly out of visual range, rising and falling with the pattern of one's gaze. Tantalus and the grapes. Or was it grapes? Water, perhaps? And what had been the offence for which that perverse incarceration was the punishment? Her ideas floated ahead of her like a conveyor-belt clothes-line decorated with pegs, but moving too fast for garments to be appended thereto. A moment of misery surged inside her head, pressing against the hard shell of her skull as the traumatized brain had.

"Tantalus," she said, more urgently.

"I know bugger-all about Tantalus," he said comfortably, clattering clean plates. "Nothin'. Empty. White sheet."

Catching the demand in her face, he closed his eyes to dredge for memories.

"I presume Tantalus is the guy who gave rise to the word 'tantalize'," he speculated. "Same as yer man that couldn't push the stone up the hill. Sisyphus. Tantalus had some equivalently frustrating exercise that he couldn't quite fulfil. I'll look it up in the library when we go out."

She sat silently, the front of her legs beginning to be too warm in the fire-heat. He would not remember to look it up, she knew, and she would not remember to remind him. And if she later reproached him, he would laugh and tell her he had more important things to be doing.

"Now, tell me where these go," he said, kicking off the wheelchair brake and pushing her towards the Christmas tree. Her legs cooled down and she nodded her instructions as to where the tinsel baubles should go. Pain was riveting the bones of her face.

"Don't grind your teeth. Makes you look like Desperate Dan in the *Dandy*," he said.

She watched him open two capsules and empty them into a flat soup spoon filled with yogurt.

He fed the sour mixture to her. A great shudder ran through her at the taste, knocking her plastered legs together and forcing one rigid forearm off the arm of the wheelchair. He lifted the arm back into position without comment.

Nor did he make predictions about the painkiller, as her mother would have done.

"You'll feel the good of that in just a few minutes," her mother would always say. "You'll never notice the time passing."

Having dosed her as neatly as a farmer dosing a sheep, he went off to get logs, stepping into Wellington boots at the door before heading out into the rainy backyard. For a moment she was filled with fear that the butterflies would follow him out the open door and wilt in the cold outside air, but they stayed where they were. He came back to build up the fire with the sure-handed enjoyment he took in any physical task. He sat back on his hunkers, his hands palmed towards the blaze.

Then the boots were shoved off and he heel-padded in socked

feet to wash his hands. One of the butterflies settled on the hot tap, and he tipped it with the back of his hand to get it away.

"Needn't have bothered our arses buying decorations," he said, half to himself. "Free butterflies ..."

The pain was beginning to ease, keeping in time with her pulse as it retreated.

"Here," he said. "Hold these."

The lightness of the box put into her lap mimicked paper. She pushed with her caged hand at the lid until it came up and off and fell to the floor. The sound of it was swamped in a sudden loud rigour of Gregorian chant from the record player. Her husband's voice joined those of the choir.

"Lumen ad revelationem gentium ..."

Six bright silver balls sat, segregated, egg-fashion, in the box, reflecting back six fattened faces at her. Even through the distortion of the convex mirroring, she could see that the face was not the one she knew: nose tilted at an angle, forehead dented, the dent rimmed by pale raised scarring. A squealing whimper came through her clenched teeth and the six reflections blurred. Her husband, unhearing, came back to the wheelchair, still singing, and began – deftly – to hook skinny wire hooks onto the baubles.

"Jesus," he said, breaking off from the male voices. "Don't *dribble* on the bloody things. Oh. You're crying. Why're you crying?"

The caged hand thumped against her chin, then onto the baubles. The voices continued to sing "*Nunc dimittis servum tuum, domine*".

"Your face, is it?"

She nodded. He mopped her with the tea towel from off his shoulder.

"Yeah," he said thoughtfully, taking some of the hooked baubles and beginning to position them on the tree. "I'd forgotten you wouldn't have seen yourself since the accident."

His tone was casually observant, as if commenting on a one-degree change in external temperature or the lateness of a newspaper. She roared at him in wordless agony, bubbles forming and bursting in the gap between top and bottom teeth. He finished hanging the baubles, came back and mopped her again.

"You have a thing called keloid scarring," he said informatively. "That's why the bump on your head has a kind of a rim on it. If you really want to, later, you can have it sort of filed down. But probably if you just grew your fringe a bit longer ... Other than that, your face is going to be a bit different. But you'll get used to it. I have."

He took the now empty box off her lap and replaced it with another one. When the lid came off, it was filled with red balls, crusted with metallic grains and non-reflective. After a moment, he resumed the Gregorian chant. When the track ended, he hummed the notes again.

"Good singer always hits the notes from above," he said, quoting some college music teacher he had liked. "Never *reaches* for them ..."

You are without sympathy, she thought. You are without imagination. You lack the capacity to understand the true horror of being behind a strange distorted face, of knowing that it will never present to the outside world what you are used to it presenting. You have no patience for "talking out" of problems and your favourite phrase is "there's the status quo, and there's worse – which do you want?" You have already got used to my battered face and you will never understand why I should have a problem doing the same. It wouldn't even occur to you to say that you see my face more than I do. You simply don't empathize enough to argue it through at all.

"D'you know what I was thinking?"

Her husband was standing over her, dangling a red bauble from its hook. One of the butterflies had settled on it.

"We won't be able to have candles at all. And we'll have to be very careful with the toaster and things like that. I must rig a couple of shields to prevent these lads from getting into danger."

She held out her arms to him and he put his head down on her neck, one arm extended to take care of the butterfly. In a desperation of trust and need, she hugged him awkwardly, hiding her hospital-pale face in the always tanned warm skin of his neck.

"Now," he said, straightening up as if something had been settled, and returning to the task.

"Butterflies and Christmas. What more could we want?"

3

Teeth first

Long before I had the car crash, I had lousy teeth. My dentist found them interesting in the way a research scientist finds an obscure disease interesting. Their composition, he opined, was of something between chalk and silly putty.

When I first got teeth crowned, I thought I was set for life. I would be able to bite freely into the hardest apples, eat the toughest steak, crunch ice for pleasure. No, the dentist said, crowns were expensive and should be taken care of. My crowns, like semi-permanent pensioners, had to be minded. Even when they were minded, they kept coming loose. There would be the stage where I thought I was imagining the small degree of movement. Then the stage where I knew the movement was real, but the crown was at least in place. Last came the stage when I was fishing the crown out of sandwiches. On one occasion, in the middle of a meeting in the office with the CEO of An Post, I got heated with him, and, mid-sentence, out popped the crown, dancing across the boardroom table towards him like Tinkerbell. Grabbing for the tooth, I apologized to everybody at the meeting.

"I'm tho thorry," I told them. "Jutht lotht it. Don't let thith dithtract from the thubject under dithcuthion for a thecond. Protheed."

Because they couldn't understand what I was lisping at them, they looked at me with that extra attention you give foreigners, eyes widening with horror at the sight, centre-front in my mouth, of a grey sharpened stump that made me look like the Wicked Stepmother of the Bushman of the Kalahari. Clutching the crown, I rose to visit the Ladies for running repairs. At which point my half-slip fell off. (All subsequent meetings with An Post have been, I suspect, a little dull for the CEO. He always watches me with a covertly hopeful expression, waiting to see which bit of me will disassemble today.)

On that occasion I snuck off to the dentist, who glued it back and held a blue light to it to make the glue permanent. Six weeks later, on a trans-Atlantic flight, it fell out again, and I had to fend off helpful cabin crew who were only dying to help me find whatever it was that I had lost on the floor. "Sod off and let me find my false teeth by myself," I wanted to say, but knew it would come out as "Thod off," so contented myself with a closed-mouth smile, a finger over my lips and a side-to-side headshake.

The passenger next to me kept looking at me with mistrust, evidently suspecting that he was a witness to a new form of air rage. His constant sideways inspection made it very difficult to jam the thing (once found and with carpet fibres cleaned off it) back into place, using dampened bread as a temporary fixative.

Thereafter, whenever I had to travel anywhere, my carry-on

was always full of temporary tooth glue. It had to be in the carry-on bag. Otherwise I would face the possibility of landing at my destination, a tooth in hand rather than mouth, only to find luggage and glue on the way to Bahrain.

When the car crash happened, the steering wheel smashed crowns and real teeth alike. I spent the first year in a wheelchair, which was fine. Two crutches bad, one wheelchair good. In a wheelchair, you can carry a cup of coffee away from where you made it. On crutches, you can't carry anything, plus you get corns on the palms of your hands. When you're on crutches, people want to know what you did to yourself, whereas when you're in a wheelchair they say, Aren't You Great? Being told I was great was OK. What was not OK was the dental work that removed the damaged remains of my teeth and left me with awful pink plastic things called "partial dentures". "Partial" because I retained four of my own teeth, two on the top, two on the bottom, at the back, like lamp-posts.

"Grand," the dentist said, when he fitted the partials. "You won't know yourself."

Bloody right, I didn't know myself. Where once I had teeth (poor things, but mine own) I now had two sucking, moving, slithering bathtubs in my mouth.

If I opened my mouth without thinking, which is what human beings do all the time, the lower false teeth thing would rise as if to acknowledge applause, and I'd have to clamp my mouth closed again. It was as if I was constantly finding jokes initially funny and then deciding no, they must be dirty. The false teeth would get attached to food, so I developed this mad maiden-aunt habit of putting an index finger ostensibly on my lower lip, but in fact the finger was pressing the false teeth back down and trying to get the food free.

People thought I was vegetarian, I ate so much pasta. I gave myself a Third World liver condition through lack of protein. (Couscous on its own will do that for you.) Favourite foods like raspberries I simply gave up because the seeds would get trapped between the hard plastic and my gum, like stones trapped in a shoe. I began to lose track of what I was saying at work, distracted by the sound of the bridge clicking and convinced everybody else could hear it too.

I tried everything to keep it firm. There were horseshoe-shaped bits of cloth impregnated with some substance of reputedly maritime origin that – claimed its advertising – created a wonderful natural bond. What it actually created was a sensation that you had an old mattress in your mouth. As the day wore on, bits of the old mattress would poke out from under the edges of the false teeth and you'd find yourself chasing them with your tongue.

I also tried adhesive in tubes. This stuff you applied in a fat line of goo before clapping the teeth in your mouth. The minute you pressed your upper teeth and the bottom false teeth together, an eruption of mush came up over the edge of the false teeth. So much of it swelled out that I figured none was left where it should be. The first cup of coffee in any day proved me wrong. Whatever was still there irrevocably tainted the day's first cup of coffee with the flavour of wintergreen. Flavoured coffees were all the rage, but not flavoured with arthritis linctus.

Having tainted the coffee, the glue did nothing else. The teeth remained as upwardly mobile as a software programmer. After a few weeks of that, there was no expectation left in me that the product would deliver on its advertising. I kept the unused tube in the bathroom, wrongly convinced that I would find an alternative use for it, and got through each day, miserable when things were routine, immutably fearful of a public accident, knowing that, once you have false teeth, you are a belly laugh waiting to happen.

You begin to remember awful seaside postcard cartoons of busty bottomy middle-aged women with their teeth in a glass beside the bed. You remember the nun at school who, descending the green marble stairs with bumpy urgency, opened her mouth to issue a condemnation and lost her false teeth instead, in full view of the whole school. Clatter clatter, they went in a mad dance down the stairs in front of her, separating but coming together at the foot of the stairs like ballroom partners loyal at the last.

She had to bend and pick them up, too, because while we students would have picked up many things, a nun's fresh-fallen false teeth were a bridge too far. Picked them up, she did, keeping her mouth purse-string closed. Swept away with them clutched in the folds of her long gown.

The worst thing of all was to discover that false teeth speed up the ageing of your face. Look at George Washington on a dollar bill. See the way his lower jaw is rigid, clamped? See how old and tense it makes him look? And you know why? Because he, like every other benighted denture wearer in the world, had difficulty keeping his upper plate affixed to the upper part of his mouth and his lower plate affixed to the lower part of his mouth. There tended to be migration, let alone the danger of fallout.

So George's dentist fitted him with the latest thing. The United

States of Teeth: upper and lower plates joined at the back by a powerful spring. The strength of the spring meant that when the teeth were inserted in the good General's mouth, the upper plate was forced – hard – against his palate and upper jaw, while the lower plate was forced, equally energetically, against the gums of his lower jaw.

There was no real danger of him losing his dentures once this spring device had been brought into play. Indeed, the only real problem this innovation posed was that the wearer had to exert considerable pressure to prevent his jaws springing apart. Keeping one's mouth closed required not only a conscious and unrelenting effort, but the muscle power to support the effort.

The result, immortalized on US currency, being that Washington, every day of his later life, had to clench his teeth very firmly every waking moment if he wanted to avoid looking like a scrawny new-hatched bird, beak avidly open for any donated worm.

I had known about George Washington's dental challenge for some time, but had not related it to the issue of facial ageing. That connection was made for me by a radio documentary.

Coming up to Hallowe'en, I heard a professorial voice on radio saying that the wise women in the Middle Ages coated their broomsticks with hallucinogenic herbs, then pretended to ride them and got as high, metaphorically speaking, as kites. This, he opined, had resulted in some of them being put to death as witches. What, I thought, the blokes got envious because the local midwife was having it off with her broomstick? What killjoys.

"But losing their teeth probably played a bigger part," the professorial type went on.

I nearly drove off the road. Women in medieval Europe, he

said, by their mid twenties often had no teeth, because if you had a toothache, in the days before local anaesthesia and fillings, the options were few. Out came the teeth, and in their absence, in pulled the lips, drawstring-fashion.

"Losing your teeth means losing bone as well," the professorial type went on. "If teeth are not in the jawbone to actively work it, it erodes so many millimetres every year. Which meant the collapse of the face to the shape we associate with the caricatures of witches, their noses lengthening to meet their chins and the distance between them lessening because of bone loss."

The presenter of the programme asked if the same thing happened, these days, when someone had teeth removed and used false teeth instead.

"Of course it does," the professional type said. "False teeth just sit on top of the gum. They provide no exercise at all for the underlying bone, and it shrinks away perceptibly, year after year. This is why face-lifts are often so disastrous. The tightening of the skin emphasizes the lack of underlying bone. The facial structure is poorly related to the younger structure of the same face, so tighter skin is far from a solution. It may simply emphasize the concavity of the face: the nose hanging down to meet the upcoming chin ..."

The minute I got home, that day, I asked Tom if he thought my jaw was eroding. He looked at me with startled interest. No, he said, after a moment or two's consideration, why the hell would it be? I told him, and he lost interest immediately. History and vanity together – yawn.

"I already look older than I am," I said desperately. "Now I know that in five years I'm going to look *decades* older than I am."

[33]

"I suspect that's why we develop long-sightedness with age," he said tranquilly. "If I don't have my new reading glasses on, you look just as you looked when I met you."

This calmed me down until I realized the flaw in his line of thinking. There was a whole world of people out there with 20/20 vision and every one of them was going to witness me turning into a witch. If I didn't do something to prevent it.

"What you need is what Bunny's Russian sailor had," Tom said.

Bunny is Bunny Carr, Chairman of Carr Communications, where Tom and I work. Decades earlier, when he was a star of TV and radio, he had interviewed a surgeon who had been involved in the treatment of a critically ill Russian seaman air-lifted off a freezer-vessel hauling cod from a major fishing ground. With considerable difficulty, the sick man was taken off his ship and transferred to the hospital, where what ailed him turned out to be a burst appendix. As the surgeon scrubbed up, he instructed his junior – the student who later became a dental surgeon – to convey to the patient, before they filled him full of general anaesthesia, that if he had false teeth, they would have to come out. The student conveyed the message.

The Russian opened his mouth and unscrewed a tooth, indicating to the astonished team that every tooth in his head was made of metal and screwed tight as a drum into his jawbone. Because of the nature of communication with the Soviet Union at the time, Bunny had been unable to find out precisely what procedure had been used, which suited Bunny just fine, because he has the horrors of anything medical. Say "injection" to him without warning and he'll faint for you, every time.

"There you are now," Tom said, having reminded me of Bunny's sailor. "Go off and research dental implants. I can't believe the Russians achieved this level of expertise all on their own. Someone else must be doing them."

Sure enough, I found, dental implantation is not a new concept. Digs in ancient Egyptian and South American sites from pre-history show that millennia ago, they were trying to get loose teeth either reimplanted or replaced with hand-shaped ivory or wood substitutes. None of them worked.

In the eighteenth century, Hogarth and others drew cartoons of gouty rich matrons buying freshly extracted teeth from healthy peasants to be transplanted to their own mouths to replace their own lost teeth. Donor teeth had a poor success rate owing to the strong immune reaction of the recipient.

During the nineteenth century, there was huge investment in gold and platinum implants. One experimenter would get lucky with one patient, the tooth would take hold and once the word got out, there would be a rash of other dentists trying exactly the same thing with no success at all. The real-life example of the Russian sailor began to look dispiritingly exceptional. He might have been one of the lucky exceptions of this century, I thought.

Then a friend came through.

"Don't look at Russia," he said. "Look at Sweden. They've apparently solved the problem of making sure the metal involved in implants like your sailor's doesn't get rejected. Bone rejects most metals. I'm posting you some stuff about it."

Days later, a small glossy-papered medical book, stiffly translated from Swedish, arrived, with pictures including one of Per Ingvar Branemark, Orthopaedic Surgeon at the University of

Lund. Mr Tooth Implant. Not that the book called him that. The book never lowered itself to regard him as anything other than a major research scientist. Since I had always imagined research scientists would spend their lives studying viruses that might turn nasty and human-eating at the drop of a mutation, the notion that one of them might spend his life trying to fool bone into accepting metal implants was a surprise.

Branemark's research had started with rabbits. Doesn't everybody's research? The Swedes studied microscopic healing in the bones of bunnies. In order to observe what was happening in the bone from inside the bone, the team designed an optical chamber housed in a titanium metal cylinder, which was screwed into the rabbit's thighbone. After the experiment had gone on for a few months, they realized that the titanium cylinder had fused to the bone, in a way absolutely untypical of the mutual standoffishness of bone and metal.

The fusing was called osseointegration and immediately gave rise to speculation as to how precisely this metal, titanium, with its capacity to fuse to bone, might most creatively be used.

Someone came up with the idea of titanium screws as bone anchors for lost teeth. Initial responses being positive, further work was done. Many experiments and trials led to a way of treating the surface of the titanium to make bone like it even better.

The Swedes did animal tests and then moved on to humans. They drilled into the bone, put a "post" in place, covered it over with gum tissue, left it in place for several months, then opened up the gum and screwed a tooth into the post – much as a DIY enthusiast inserts a rawlplug into a wall surface to accept and hold on to a wood screw.

The concept and the designs were refined and further refined as the months and years passed. During this time, international dentistry was unmoved by the prospect of permanent dental implants. By the mid eighties, however, enough of the implanted patients were still chewing away to prove that the concept worked. Furthermore, the level of satisfaction expressed by the implantees was so immeasurably higher than the satisfaction expressed by false-teeth wearers – typically middling to low – that dentists, who like the rest of us ache to be popular, began to realize that this development might hold some promise.

All over the world, others began to get in on the Swedish act, designing implant systems with marginal differences in design from the original Branemark Titanium Screw.

"Dental implants are biocompatible substitutes for lost natural teeth," I told Tom the evening the booklet arrived. "They are devices for attaching artificial replacement teeth firmly to the bone. Implants can be used to support a single crown or as anchors for fixed bridges. Fixed or removable, partial or complete dentures."

"Oh, yeah," he said, reminded of something he had obviously meant to tell me. "I discovered a guy in the golf club has one. One implant. Cost him a king's ransom, he said. He had one single one put in because he got a thump in the mouth in rugby. Cost £2,500."

I ran my tongue around my mouth to work out how many teeth I would need in order to work out how many times I would need to multiply £2,500 if I were to get implants. But false teeth are all fused together, so you can't count them. I figured the bottom of my mouth might cost £25,000. I didn't have a spare £25,000.

Let's be honest, I didn't have a spare £250. But did that stop me calling Tom's pal the next day to get the name of his expensive dental implant man? You're dead right, it didn't.

Having taken the initiative, I was dismayed to find that the guy could not see me for two months. In private medicine and dentistry, the length of a surgeon's waiting list is testimony to how in-demand he or she is. If a surgeon can see you within a week or so, you can figure that this is a plonker who operates using teaspoons sharpened against the nearest concrete wall.

I made an impressed noise at the receptionist, who unbent sufficiently to promise that she would send me some information about her employer and – in deference to my mention of her boss's wonder-working with Tom's friend – further promised to telephone me about any cancellation which might open up his schedule.

A leaflet arrived forty-eight hours later. It established her boss as a student and fan of the Swedish pioneer and himself an expert in endosteal implantation – meaning he puts posts directly into bone, some long and thin, some short and stubby, their size and shape chosen in each case depending on the quality and quantity of available bone.

I read this with dismay. The "available bone" situation in my mouth was probably poor to pathetic, I decided. I went to look in the mirror. My profile was definitely taking on the witches' banana curve, chin pointing up towards drooping nose. As I shoved my face at the mirror, I noticed something else. Halfway between my mouth and my ears, there was loose skin, puckered. Like a partially deflated balloon.

"Bloody hell," I said.

People always talk about crow's feet and wrinkles, but this was much worse than wrinkles. This was a loose, deadly flabby section of skin unrelated to the movement of expression, not a pleasing semi-permanent reflection of all the times I had laughed merrily. This was just sag. If I put my fingers two inches away from my ears and moved them towards my ears, I could flatten out the saggy bit, but only by moving half an inch of leftover skin back to my hairline. The moment I let go – whoof. Down it came again. Crinkled like the bark of a tree. Crumpled like the skin of an elephant. Nothing that a good moisturizer would solve. I had noticed, every now and again, that my skin was less elastic at the end of a tiring day. This had not been a tiring day, and we were only just past noon, anyway. This looked grimly permanent. However, that's another day's work, I decided, I'll deal with the teeth first.

"You sure you want a pneumatic drill digging holes in your bones?" Tom asked.

"Implant academies and associations around the world have conducted long-term studies. In addition, participants at the Harvard School of Dental Medicine Conference on Dental Implants have endorsed dental implant techniques as safe and effective," I read aloud from one of the leaflets.

"Well, they would say that, wouldn't they?" he replied.

A few weeks later, in the waiting room before me on the day of my appointment were two people: the famous wife of a major rock star, and a tiny little housewife who looked as if being in the same room with the famous one was making her hyperventilate. When Wife Of got called into the room next door, the housewife asked me if I'd yet had implants. No, I said. Just considering them.

"Oh, you have to do it," she said earnestly. "They'll change your life. I haven't been as happy since I was married first."

"Because of dental implants?"

"Oh, yes, love."

"Happy?"

"Oh, yes, love. For twenty years, I couldn't chew comfortably. I just had to stop eating first one thing that I liked and then another. Nuts was the first, then meat. Then crackers and crisp cookies. Then anything with seeds in. It was just an agony, every day. My husband used to say I was going to end up like a little granny before I was forty, eating bread dipped in hot milk, and it was true. I wouldn't say there was a week in all the twenty years that I didn't have an ulcer somewhere under my false teeth, hurting so much, love, you'd cry. And if you ate anything salty – oooh. No relations, either."

I couldn't work out what this meant.

"To be perfectly frank with you," she added, blushing.

I was still at a loss.

"No lovemaking, dear," she explained, kindly.

"Why not?"

"Well, I'd be in such agony all day, once night fell, I was so glad to get them out, wasn't I, and I couldn't have my husband making love to me gummy, so we just agreed to put it to one side, you know? But my husband, he says, since the implants, everything's come right and that it's like riding a bicycle, you never lose the knack. Mortgaged the house, he did, and no complaint. Thirty-five thousand. More than we paid for the house twenty years ago when we got married, although of course, inflation and everything has affected house prices. But he took out a new mortgage and no complaint, because he says when the kids were small, I couldn't have done this, now's my time. He says anyway it's good for both of us. It's changed my life back to what it was when I was twenty. No – better than what it was when I was twenty."

Wife Of reappeared and headed for the outer door. Little Mrs Implant was called next. She beamed at me and disappeared into the inner sanctum. For just a moment, I wondered if he laid her on (so to speak) to encourage patients to invest, but then I realized that a dentist with a month-long waiting list for a procedure that required you to take out a second mortgage would not actually need cheerleaders planted in his waiting room.

Before I got invited into the inner sanctum, I must have a dental X-ray, I was told. I considered protesting but decided they would probably need to know if I had any real bone left in my face into which you could anchor a tooth or two, so I caved in and agreed to it.

First of all, they put me in this thing like a circular telephone box or one of those tiny round saunas you can install in your own home. Then they put a lead apron on me and fitted my chin into a kind of apparatus like the one they used in medieval times when they wanted to pelt the village idiot with overripe tomatoes or whatever produce was going a-begging. I held my chin on this, like someone in the stocks, and they retreated behind protective walls to activate machinery that came from one side of the sauna, stopped, went to the other, came back and stopped with a jolt.

The bad bit of all this is that I had to take out my partial dentures, first. I sneaked them into a tissue and the X-rays were taken with my mouth firmly closed. At least, unlike photographs, X-rays can be taken through skin.

I'm sneaking the partial dentures back into my mouth when an international soccer star comes out of a room off this central area, flashes me a confident smile and exits. I sit, picking bits of tissue off the partial in my mouth with my tongue, wondering if he's had implants.

When I get into the chair in front of the surgeon, I ask "What kind of people do well with implants?" hoping the surgeon will say "Well, you saw Head-the-Ball on the way out of here? He's had 39 put in since Bukonevsky hit him full-frontally in the face with the penalty in the X match." He never mentions Head-the-Ball, though.

"Most patients who are healthy enough to undergo normal dental treatment and maintain good oral hygiene can have dental implants," he says, primly as a maiden aunt giving out about a littered sitting-room. "Occasionally, we come across specific health conditions or structures of the mouth that prevent successful implantation. But this would not apply in your case."

Aha, I think, the syphilitic lesions haven't been noticed.

He sits down beside me and palms his hands together between his knees, boyishly. Boyishness in a man the wrong side of fifty is quite unnerving, but maybe witch-prevention makes dental implanters feel youthful.

"Tell me what you would want dental implants to achieve for you, Terry," he says gently.

Oh, bloody hell, I think. He's trying to assess if my expectations are excessive. Do I believe the implants will make me look thirteen and a half, double my salary and see me pulling toy-boys off bus-queues?

"They would prevent me having to take out false teeth when I have to have a general anaesthetic," I say.

"Do you often have general anaesthetics?"

"No. Hardly ever. But if I was, I wouldn't want the humiliation."

"Humiliation" proves to be a kind of trigger word. He does a five-minute monologue about the humiliation associated with false teeth and at the end of it has convinced himself that, psychologically, I'm sound as a pound and we should head straight for the operating theatre. To tackle our lower jaw. (Body parts become collective when you spend time with medics, I notice.) His nurse suggests a date two weeks away. His impressive waiting time must apply only to newcomers. Once you have qualified as worth implanting, it happens without undue delay. I absorb the details. There will be a two-to-three-night stay in the clinic. Costs? There's the cost of the nights at the clinic, for starters. Then there's the cost of the general anaesthetic and of the prosthesis. Plus his boyish hand on the dagger.

When I do a rough tot, I find that getting a lower jaw filled with implants is likely to set me back £25,000, and I won't see results for a year.

But by now I have convinced myself that dental implants will prevent me turning into a witch, my chin curling up to meet my nose, will prevent draw-string wrinkles forming around my lips, remove the mortification of false teeth, their glues, smells, fizzy-pill cleaners, gag-awful jokes and gothic noises, and allow me to bite into a hard apple, tackle a raw turnip, savage a steak and chew brazil nuts at will.

To be sure, I hate apples, never eat turnip raw or cooked and am ambivalent at best about steak and nuts. But I have noticed that one of the deadly age-giveaways is apple-behaviour. Getting old starts, frequently, in the mouth. Hand someone an apple, and if age has already stricken them, they will either refuse it and go for the easier mushier option of a banana, pear or bunch of grapes, or they will want to address it with a knife.

Give a young person an apple, on the other hand, and they just bite. The big apple-bite has become a Proustian trigger. The hell with madeleines. Madeleines are for those whose teeth are already gone. But a hard apple, insouciantly bitten, evokes youth, sensuality and unplanned sex. Well, youth, anyway. Maybe the unplanned sex happens more with peach-juice running down the chin ...

In the interest of apple-biting and witch-avoidance, I borrow from the credit union, expand an overdraft, promise a number of economies and enter the clinic.

I come up from the general anaesthetic with a huge wad of something in my mouth and a great desire to (a) spit it out and (b) lie down. Or the reverse order. But they keep explaining that I have to bite down on the gauze and I must not lie down because I will choke on the gauze.

I bite and sleep (sitting up) and get the same instructions from about eight nurses. Staff turnover seems awfully high, I explain to Tom at one point: eight nurses succeeding each other over as many hours indicating low levels of job satisfaction.

"I can't make out what you're saying," Tom says. "So don't waste your time. You want to bite on ice?"

I nod and he gives me some. Biting down on it feels wonderful. I gesture towards my face.

"What do you look like?" Tom gives this more consideration than it deserves. "Lopsidedly beaten up," he eventually offers.

[44]

"Like a lefty beat the shit out of you. Your jaw on one side is swollen to twice its size and filled with a saggy bruise. Plus you have a black eye and he must have dropped something on your chest because you're bruised there, too."

This makes unexpected sense. One of the odd characteristics I have noticed about this dental surgeon is that, like a motor mechanic used to someone tidying up after them, he simply drops his tools on the handiest surface, which five times out of ten is my chest. Since I have a somewhat bony upper chest, they often make quite a rattle as they land, but he never seems to notice. It seems a little disrespectful to a patient paying £25,000 for implants to use their torso as a toolbox, but there doesn't seem to be any personal malice in it, so I have not complained. He probably, I tell Tom, dropped heavier things on me under the cover of the general anaesthetic. Tom looks at me blankly, not having understood a word I have said.

"You're out of your mind, you know," he says, examining my appearance all over again. "Putting yourself through this just to avoid dentures."

"False teeth," I correct, but he thinks I am agreeing with him and begins to console me for my mistakes. I gesture towards the door and off he goes, leaving me with my bruised chest and my mouthful of gauze.

The following day, gauze removed, I can feel hard protrusions beneath my gums. These, I learn, are the posts. The dental surgeon has bored holes and depressions in my partial denture so it will fit over the new arrivals, because of my insistence on going back to work.

The nurse tells me of an unnamed romantic novelist who is the doctor's patient, too. Said novelist is simply staying indoors for the nine months until the next phase of the implants. That's by far the best option, the nurse explains, because the romantic novelist will not have to wear false teeth. She can go gummy around the house and because she will be eating on her gums, this will work the posts, stimulate the gums and it will all be very satisfactory.

I go back to work resigned to eating mush, and am delighted to find that the partial denture is a million times more secure and comfortable with the posts poking into the holes the dentist has made in it. The months which have to elapse between the first and second stages begin to look much more pleasant. I'm out of the wheelchair and trying to teach myself not to limp. Which isn't easy, when one of your legs is considerably shorter than the other.

Being mobile and beginning to be able to eat sensibly makes me feel better, so I begin to write again. Weight-loss begins to happen. In the past, when I lost weight, my face got thinner and better looking. Now, presumably because I'm coming up to forty years of age, my face gets baggier. The loose, almost invisibly puckered quality of my facial skin, allied to the fact that my face is lopsided, anyway, since the accident, gives me a jolt every time I catch sight of myself in a window or a mirror.

My skin now has that defeated look an apple gets when it is somewhere between ripe and rotten. I find myself comparing those apples with brand-new apples. The over-ripe ones will be sweet inside, but the look of them can't compare with the taut shiny health of a Golden or Red Delicious, hard and polishable against one's trousers.

Remembering the man on the radio programme who said face-lifts were only half-effective because of bone loss in the underlying facial structure, it strikes me that perhaps they are twice as effective once you have ensured that the underlying bone structure stops eroding. If they are twice as effective, my thinking continues, would it not be something of a waste to have dental implants and not to at least consider, at least do a little research into the possibilities of, a face-lift?

Accordingly, but purely, you understand, with a view to making these implants cost-effective, as the first stage of the healing and osseointegration begins, I embark on some sneaky research about plastic surgery. Just out of curiosity ...

4

Sneaky research into plastic surgery

I think it was William James who said that the most fundamental human need is to be appreciated.

Amend that, for plastic surgeons.

For plastic surgeons, the most basic human need is to be appreciated for more than prettifying people. Now, you might have thought prettifying people was an honourable enough career, but you'd be wrong. Plastic surgeons *hate* being the surgical equivalent of pastry cooks in a restaurant kitchen. So they develop a defensive double-whammy:

1. "I'm better qualified than Others Who Shall Be Nameless but who are not even –" (tooth-sucking, head-shaking, voice-lowering disgust) "– Board-*certified*."

2. "Plastic surgery is not modern superficiality. It goes back a long, long time ..."

Claim 1 surfaces all the time.

Once you begin to look at the possibility of getting your face raised a little, you get your nose rubbed in the competing qualifications of the people who might operate the elevator. Every lecture is larded with references, every surface littered with leaflets which leave you with the absolute conviction that there's a bunch of half-qualified carpet-steamers, landscape gardeners and jobbing electricians moonlighting as plastic surgeons.

Caveat emptor on steroids is what it feels like. You want to know will they make you young and beautiful. They want to warn you about Joe Bloggs the kerb-layer who has set up a clinic down the road. They give you lists of surgeons who belong to their association. They give you cards with 800 numbers on to call to ease your mind.

All of which has a result exactly the reverse of what they hope. You begin to think to your wrinkly little self, "Hey, if I have a meal in a restaurant, the head waiter doesn't give me a health warning about other eateries where the cooking is done by bicycle-repair guys in their spare time. Before we get to the qualifications, Doctor, any chance you'd show us the menu? Tell us what you can actually achieve?"

Except that the moment you get them off their crying jag about underqualified scalpel-swingers, they segue straight into a point-by-point proof that plastic surgery wasn't born yesterday. So? When we go buy a car, do we get told about the links between this model and the carts found frozen in lava in Pompeii?

It's as if they want to compete with prostitutes to be recognized as the oldest profession in the world. They can't wait to tell you that the term "plastic" has no connection at all with that nasty cheap stuff that followed Bakelite as a material for knobs on radios and handles for saucepans. Perish the thought that plastic surgery would be categorized in anybody's mind with the cheap, the spurious, the artificial.

Let us, rather, associate it with antiquity and the classics. Because the plastic referred to comes from the Greek *plastica*, meaning to form or mould.

The other thing plastic surgeons nearly always want to impress you with is how valuable their work is to the injured and deformed. That, after all, is where the art began, they will tell you. It was practised as early as 1500 BC in India. There, women's noses, mutilated by jealous husbands (or fathers, who had the right to disfigure them if they suspected them of infidelity), were reconstructed using flaps of skin from the forehead.

One is supposed to be rendered wide-eyed and speechless by this info. The first time it was presented to me, I was puzzled, figuring that there was a missing link in the story. Imagine the pre-historic Indian woman who fancies the contemporary equivalent of the travelling salesman. Or is believed by her husband to fancy someone other than the husband. This woman is so subservient that the husband can amputate her nose without any fear of the law. Seems to me that so subservient a woman is not likely to have a separate income source or the autonomy to decide, a week or so after her face has had its central feature removed, "OK, now let's go have a reconstruction done."

If the surgery was not paid for by some form of health insurance scheme, was it the mutilating husbands who paid for it? Never mind the morality – it was poor value for money over a lifetime, I'd have thought. You knock the nose off your wife, then pay for it to be reconstructed ("Now you've learned your lesson, you can have a new one") and then, in the nature of things, pre-decease her so she ends up, expensive nose-job and all, being incinerated on your funeral pyre.

Anyway, what's *with* noses in history? For aeons, the human race seems to have been nose-focused to an extraordinary degree. Never mind foot-fetishists: in olden days, a glimpse of nostril seems to have been where it was at. No matter where you lived, if you were female, the bit of your anatomy in pretty constant danger seems to have been your nose, removal of which was the ultimate censure, achieving two objectives at one blow: notify the community, scarlet-letter-fashion, that you've been sleeping around, and at the same time render you so unattractive as to radically reduce your chances of sleeping around in future.

Even in Renaissance Italy, when surgeon Gaspar Tagliacozzi wrote the first textbook of plastic surgery, he lovingly described the taking of a skin flap from the arm, for use in the reconstruction of a missing nose. Not that the Italians were necessarily knocking hell out of their womenfolk. I suspect the missing Italian noses may have been eaten away by syphilis, arriving back to the home-land courtesy of travellers like the Crusaders. Another enemy of the nose would have been leprosy, not then called Hansen's Disease and still fearful in its capacity to erode limbs and features.

One way or the other, Italy, in the Middle Ages, saw enough nose-jobs to win friend Gaspar quite a reputation. The city of Bologna summed it all up, sculpturally, by erecting a statue of him – holding a detached nose in his hand. Can you imagine a modern city putting up a statue of a plastic surgeon, holding a lifted face?

At least these days, when people go to plastic surgeons, it tends to be because age has done them subtle damage over time. Plastic surgery patients in history tended to have suffered more visible, immediate damage by a passing scimitar or axe. Lopping lugs or hacking off hands could serve as notice to the public that the individual missing the odd bit of his or her anatomy might be a miscreant. Sort of a public health warning. *Associating with this nose-free person can cause loss of status, loss of income and maybe loss of life ...* It's difficult to plan a career-path if you carry that kind of warning in the middle of your face. For PR purposes alone, a repair job was indicated.

Of course, if you were a thief, rather than a sexually active spouse, the powers-that-were might remove a hand, rather than a nose. A hell of a deterrent, this. Not just the shame factor, although that must have been profound. Difficult to impress a new client with your warm handshake, and inevitable that any prospective client will go "Whoa – do I want to deal with a convict?" There was also the more practical deterrent that a thief missing a hand or two is a little short of the tools of his trade.

The socially advantageous side of this slash-and-tear style of moral correction lay in its value as a training ground for the plastic surgeons of the day. Those surgeons got to do reconstructive work on people who had been unjustly punished. Such a consolation it must have been for the amputees to know they were contributing to the refinement of medical knowledge.

The best thing that ever happened to plastic surgery was the First World War, when, for the first time, it began to be seen as a legitimate branch of surgery. "Plastic Surgery Units" were opened in British hospitals for the first time, designed to treat combat veterans with extensive gunshot injuries and burns.

This was made possible by developments in anaesthesia and antiseptics.

Until anaesthetics were invented, what distinguished the great surgeon from the average surgeon was speed. If you had to have surgery when you couldn't be knocked out for it and when your skin could not be deadened by a local anaesthetic, you desperately needed a speedy surgeon to limit the excruciating agony by getting through the procedure quickly.

Of course, once anaesthesia was available, the Speedy Gonzalezes of surgery were effectively de-skilled and the slow guys came into their own. If the patient was asleep, the patient felt nothing, and so it no longer mattered whether an operation took two minutes or two hours.

Sadly, just as anaesthesia was becoming more sophisticated, so too were weapons of war. Sub-machine guns could create human damage – in survivors – the like of which had never been seen before. The extent and complexity of the injuries presented to European surgeons who had never before seen anything so dreadful, tested their ingenuity and inventiveness. A warm and positive public reaction to the results achieved by plastic surgeons on the war-wounded reinforced their position.

A French army surgeon named Morestin was one of the first to show that skin and the underlying tissue could be pulled back (as in a face-lift) without necrosis – tissue death – as an inevitable consequence. The techniques he developed were originally designed to cope with the large number of patients with gunshot wounds to the face coming into military hospitals during the war, many of whom transferred to his special treatment centre.

Two British surgeons in France at that time were so impressed by what they saw that, after the war, they returned home to set up a unit at Aldershot Military Hospital, which was to serve as the nucleus of a centre of facial plastic surgery at the Queen Mary Hospital, Sidcup, Kent.

The term "plastic surgery" not only became popularly understood in a very short space of time, but began to emerge in the titles of textbooks like *Plastic Surgery: Its Principles and Practice*, published in 1919. In the United States, around the same time, general surgeons were beginning to experiment with cosmetic surgery, pioneering reconstructive work to correct birth defects or damage from accidents, diseases or war injuries. By the 1920s there was a move towards "improving" facial features rather than simply correcting gross deformities. This started with the "bobbing" of a famous actress's nose. Before long, people outside show business were asking for their noses to be bobbed in imitation of Fanny Brice's. (Ironically, Fanny Brice, several generations later, was to be played on screen by Barbra Streisand, who not only refused to have her distinctive, even assertive, nose bobbed, but made it central to her brand image.)

By the thirties, the assumption that you were stuck with the looks you were born with was beginning to be questioned, as was the assumption that you should live with whatever damage age did to your appearance. The first few rudimentary face-lifts on patients who were getting older and who were scared that, if it showed, they might lose their jobs, marked the start of the belief that while you couldn't hold back the clock, you could improve the clock face.

This, despite the fact that some of the early facial-improvement techniques were disastrous. One such technique became known as the Paraffin Menace. In the beginning, it seemed a dream scheme: patients who had developed puckered wrinkles around the mouth, for example, could have their wrinkles smoothed and the deflated area plumped up again with injections of paraffin wax. The setting of the wax would, it was believed, solve the problem. Except that on occasion the wax would set and then shift, and on too many occasions the entire area would become grievously inflamed and painful, with loss of tissue and permanent deformity.

Despite the disasters, people whose jobs depended on them looking good/young were willing to go (quietly) under the plastic surgeon's knife in increasing numbers. In the fifties and sixties, the odd gossip column might observe that a star like Lucille Ball seemed to be looking younger these days – so much younger that there's a danger her eyebrows might disappear into her hair – but if Lucille, like Brer Rabbit, was lyin' low and sayin' nothin', there wasn't much more the columnists could do about it.

In that context, comedienne Phyllis Diller was the first major exception. Never having had beauty to start with, she had no authenticity to defend. So, when she had her first face-lift, she went public about it and almost made viewing it a part of her act. She had no problem about before-and-after photographs. The Before shots showed her as an astonishingly wrinkled forty-year-old. The After shots showed her damn near smooth, and better-looking, rather than younger-looking.

Suddenly, the traditional arguments against face-lifts didn't seem so valid. Why in the name of God, people began to think, would anyone want to look like the Before if they could choose to look like the After?

Phyllis Diller went on to have dozens of surgical interventions of the plastic sort. Oh, went the comments as the photographs of her arrived on editorial desks, doesn't she look dreadful? No, was the answer. She doesn't look dreadful. Odd, yes. Dreadful, no.

If she had started off as beautiful, it would be easy to judge the repair job. If successful, it would bring her back, or nearly back, to her original good looks. But when the starting point is decayed homeliness, and when the plastic surgeon changes that to near-prettiness, it makes the observer do a double-take.

Which gives one to think. If someone who has always looked like the back end of a truck is going to put down the money needed for a face-lift, should that person confine her demands and expectations to what life doled out originally? Should she go for a repair job that makes her look like a younger version of the back end of a truck, or is it legitimate to say to a surgeon: "Don't just give me young, give me beautiful too"?

The drawback to radical redesign, as opposed to running repairs, is that you can keep your mouth shut about why you're looking so rested, but it's difficult to be silent about why you look so different your own kids don't know you. And there's a lot to be said for silence. As I'm doing basic research into plastic surgeons and plastic surgery, it's all over the papers that Julie Christie has admitted to having had a face-lift. I haven't seen a single inter-view or profile since that hasn't mentioned it. She used to be Julie Christie, symbol of Swinging London, or Julie Christie, Dr Zhivago's bird, or Julie Christie, fine actress. Now she's Julie Christie, recent face-lift.

I can't, at this stage, figure I would ever be the sort of person who had a face-lift. But I'm certain of one point. If I did have one, I'd never, *ever*, admit to it.

5

Mr Surgeon, what was your worst result?

When I'm doing my sneaky research into plastic surgery, it strikes me that the great advantage dental implants have over something like a face-lift is that you never have to explain them. Dental work is either uninteresting to others, or provokes them to tell you about their most recent experience in the dentist's chair.

The minute you say "dental complications", someone says, with a shudder, "Oh, root canal? Listen, I had ..." and off they go on their most recent experience. So, going back to work quickly after the first implant procedure was no problem. I just used lots of pan-stick make-up to conceal the yellowing bruises on my face, and wore a polo-neck to hide the chest-bruise where the surgeon had dumped his toolbox or spanner. Nobody wanted to know the details.

The day I went back to work, the first thing I noticed on my desk was an envelope fat with photographs taken by the former

Health Minister Gemma Hussey. Gemma runs an organization that promotes democracy in the former Iron Curtain countries, bringing women journalists and parliamentarians to Ireland to learn about the joys and miseries of a free press. One or two days of the week-long visit are usually spent in Carr Communications, where we give them the rudiments of media presentation skills.

I look through Gemma's pictures, identifying individuals from Romania, Croatia, Poland. Towards the end, there's one of me, in full flight. I'm surrounded by women dressed unglamorously for work, concentrating hard on someone talking in a foreign language, but, *Gawd*, even in a nobody-wins-the-prize-for-beauty situation, I still came out worst. I look animated, confident and – old. Brightly dressed, brightly made up – like an old tart. Like one of the ugly sisters in a pantomime: full of awful energy, jowls a-wag.

I decide to burn the dress in which I had been photographed, horrified at the way the narrow belt neatly separated the rounded spare tire above my waist from the little pot belly below the belt. Admittedly, these pictures were taken when I was sitting down, but to hell with that as an excuse.

If I go higher than spare-tire level, I get an eyeful of stringy neck. My mother always told me that if I lost weight my neck would go stringy, and here it is, the justification of her predictions. I've now lost 90 pounds, post accident, mainly because I want to look good for the publicity around the launch of a book of short stories. I figure that because literary short stories do not attract much attention, I should help the collection along. So I eat bloody broccoli for six months solid, and what's the result? Nobody gives a toss about the short stories (*Blood Brothers, Soul Sisters*, still in print, and described by David Marcus as the most impressive debut in a decade) but everybody wants a copy of my diet sheet.

Now, thinner, I look bitterly at Gemma's photographs, talking to myself. You lost all that weight and two dress sizes. You keep meeting people who saw you on TV after the diet, and they always greet you with "Oh, I see you kept the weight off." It's like doing the goddam Leaving Cert on a weekly basis. You are a hero. And then Gemma takes snapshots, and there's the payoff for all your effort: stringiness. Two empty folds of skin, starting under the chin, going down the lower neck.

I pull out a mirror, thinking: "Maybe I was tired. Maybe the pictures were taken late in the day." Maybe, in short, the wattles are not there under my chin. Maybe the implants were already working in some magical way to – no, they are certainly there. The wattles. Large as life and twice as repulsive.

That, I decide, is because my face isn't fit. You know those exercise pads you can paste to your stomach that'll give you the equivalent of 150 sit-ups electrically? They now have got a little battery version for the face. Pulls up all the loose lazy bits, gets the circulation going, eliminates jowls – wondrous, my dear. Hundred bucks. Cheap at the price, I decide, and mail-order one.

It comes with lotion but no batteries, so I buy batteries and sit down to try it out. It tickles my skin like a lit match. I go back and read the instructions. The lotion, says the instructions, increases the conductivity between the flat plates of the gadget and the face. I try the lotion. The waspy stinging subsides but nothing else seems to be happening when the machine is applied to my face. I turn up the power. One side of my face goes into spasm. I haul the thing away and turn the power back down.

In front of a mirror, I experiment with different settings: 1–2 gives a sensation like mild pins and needles; 3–4 creates a little tweaking of facial muscles; 5–7 evokes spasmodic changes of expression; 7–10 contorts the face into terrifying tangles of bunched skin and brainless lewd grimaces.

The machine comes with an egg-timer, so you exercise each section of your face for the appropriate length of time only. I suppose nobody wants to develop ropy jaw muscles the way weight-trainers develop ropy biceps. There are something like twelve different points on the face and neck, each earning itself two minutes of electric stimulation. That's twenty-four minutes.

Half an hour in the evenings and mornings will be no problem. Wrong. Getting out of bed a half an hour earlier is fine – until the alarm clock goes off. After a couple of days, I decide the best time to do this is in the car going to work. I figure onlookers will assume it's a carphone. They do. One of the guys in the office, who, in a traffic jam, spots me using it, tells everybody he saw me clearly having telephone sex with someone.

"Orgasm by facial expression," he announces at the water cooler and does a performance without words that makes Meg Ryan's fake orgasm in *When Harry Met Sally* look like frigidity. I am so embarrassed, I produce the little massager and let them all try it. They use up the batteries, making their foreheads jump up and down.

"I wanted to have a fit face," I say. "But all it's achieved so far for me is to stimulate a bundle of nervous tics, so I'm winking and twitching all day long. Plus Tom finds it distracts him from sport on television to have a wife who is exercising one side of her face with what looks to him like the TV remote-control device."

I did keep it up for at least two months, for all the good it did me. The leaflet that came with the little machine had a before-and-after photograph of this woman in profile. In the first shot she had a noticeable double chin and jowls. In the second, she had a profile off a Greek coin. It said "unretouched photograph" but who is going to check? A fashion correspondent friend later told me she had seen an old version of the machine, produced perhaps twenty years earlier, and the pictures being used to publicize it were the same ones of the woman with the double chin and the jowls that disappeared. Unretouched, of course. I bitterly conclude that Helga or Irmgaard, or whatever the hell is the name of this photographed woman, was the only success story they ever had.

The problem is that I have another new book coming out. A novel, this time. Which means getting publicity pictures taken. I can feel my wattles trembling at the thought. That night, Tom comes home to find me lying on the kitchen floor looking at myself in a mirror.

"This is how I want to look in the book-launch photograph," I explain. "I was reading a feature in a magazine that this is how you look when you've had a good face-lift."

"Presumably, if you've had a *really* good face-lift, you can even stand up?" Tom suggests, stepping over me to get to the kettle.

"Lying down on your back allows gravity to work for you rather than against you," I state, letting him help me to my feet.

"Oh, now you're upright, gravity is pulling your cheeks towards the floor?" he speculates, looking at me with a new interest.

"You're nearer the truth than you know," I say grimly.

"So you're gonna have a face-lift before the book launch next month?"

"There isn't time, but I have a cunning plan."

I show him the magazine advert. Secret of Hollywood Stars, it says. As good as a face-lift, but without surgery. There is a before-and-after sequence of shots with this, too. In the Before shot, the woman looks wrinkled and depressed. In the After shot, she looks smooth and cheery.

I send off for the product. It arrives in a plain wrapper and is complicated as all hell. There are little transparent tabs of plastic in roughly the shape of luggage tags, one side smooth, the other slightly rough, and at one end a hole for you to thread something through. The "something" is elastic thread, in black, brown, yellow or white, depending on your hair colour.

Once you have the elastic threaded through one of the tabs, you wet the rough side, thus activating a heavy-duty glue, and stick it to a part of your face. I stick it to my cheekbone. Then you stick another tab on the other side of your face, thread the other end of the elastic through it, and knot it in your hair, ensuring that the elastic pulled both tabs simultaneously towards the back of your head. The glue provides resistance, and so your face gets pulled back towards your ears. You stick other tabs under your jaw and loop the elastic over the top of your head, and a final set at your temples.

The first thing I learn is that if I put the tabs too far forward on my face, the elastic pulls so over-enthusiastically, I can't close my eyes. I can't open them fully, either. I'm like a Chinese in a semi-coma. That's the effect of tabs at the temple and cheekbones.

If I over-tighten the ones at my temple, it gives me the expression you'd expect of someone who has just seen the Ghost of Christmas Past.

On the other hand, a couple of tabs just under my hair at the neck pull the wattles completely away from the front of my neck. It also, however, gives me an ongoing mild sensation of suffocation and a desire to do that forefinger job men do to loosen too-tight shirt collars.

Once you have the tabs stuck in place, the final task is to either pull tendrils of your hair over them to conceal them, or to make up your face so they are concealed. There are two complications in this ostensibly simple task. The first is that you cannot make up plastic to look like skin. The other is that if you have always worn your hair pulled straight back, ballerina-style, it's difficult to suddenly make with the tendrils.

I try the make-up route. It makes me look as if someone has thrown flesh-coloured Elastoplast at me in a random way. Tendrils of hair it would have to be, I decide. Except that I have now run out of gummed stickies. Time for tab-recycling. Hey, environmentally friendly fake face-lifts. I wash the tabs thoroughly – which is not easy, since at this point they have dried-out glue on one side and make-up on the other – and try them again, this time using superglue.

It works perfectly, as do the tendrils. The only problem is that, having superglued them on, I can't get them off. At all. As a consequence, I have all-day, all-night tabs for about a week. At bedtime, I undo the elastic thread and sleep with the untethered tabs in place. You can get quite used to this. They are a bit noisy scratching against the pillow, but other than that pose no problem.

The day they launched my novel *Racing the Moon*, I got so anxious about the capacity of my newly trimmed tendrils to cover up the tabs that I ended up supergluing the tendrils to the tabs, forgetting that I would want to move my head right and left. Anchored by superglued tendrils, this was hard to do. During the day, people kept asking me if I had a crick in my neck, although they did also tell me I looked wonderful. I had that tight-skinned look you get wearing a bathing cap that is marginally too small for you or a pony-tail so firmly rubber-banded it gives you a look of ironed astonishment.

I did keep shying away from people, though. Up close, you could see the faint outline of the tabs, and I was terrified someone would ask me why I had sellotape holding the sides of my face on. On the night of the launch, I was interviewed on radio by Vincent Browne, the mongoose of Irish journalism. His opening question was something to the effect that when I can produce work of literary merit and run a company which has a household name, why do most people think I'm a bimbo? My mother was livid. The *idea*, she kept saying. I don't understand why you're not *furious*, she would add. I couldn't tell her that I was so afraid Vincent might notice my sticky bits and reveal all to his listening audience that being called a bimbo was – by comparison – almost welcome.

"You going to buy another instalment of those face things?" Tom asked when I came home from the radio studio and began to peel them and half my skin off. I shook my head.

"That's a relief," he said. "In bed, when you're asleep, you remind me of a package with tabs to open it with. Too much trouble, are they?"

I nodded. He didn't say it, but his expression conveyed the message: "Glad you're getting sense."

Except I was not getting sense. I was thinking back to the ad that had first attracted me to the tabs-and-elastic system. "A face-lift without surgery," it had said. I had tried it. The pictorial results were splendid. I looked lovely. Wattle-free.

Maybe it was time to think of a face-lift *with* surgery. That thought would have to be put on hold, I figured, until after a business trip I had to make to Florida the following week. Of course, just as, once you decide not to think of a pink elephant, the world abounds in pink-elephant references, the minute I had resolved not to think about a face-lift, face-lift references were everywhere.

The book I bought to tide me over the two flights was Rita Mae Brown's autobiography, *Rita Will.* Towards the end of the book is a section devoted to a former girlfriend of Martina Navratilova – a very pretty woman who, after she parts with Martina (and parts Martina from a goodly chunk of palimony), has a face-lift.

"It doesn't matter how much you tart yourself up; if you're fifty-two, you're fifty-two," writes Rita Mae about her own reaction to the surgery. "You might look like a great fifty-two, but why try to look young? Let the young have it. We had our shot."

Whoa, Rita Mae, I said in my own mind. (She's very into horses, is Rita Mae, so this cry would make sense to her.) Maybe the lady didn't want to look young. Maybe she *just* wanted to look "a great fifty-two" but couldn't look a great fifty-two with spare saggy skin on her face? I don't want to look thirty. I just want to look a great forty-two, and see these wattles here, Rita Mae? Not even weightlifting like you do with such discipline is going to take them away.

Having taken care of her first point, I went back to reading, only to find that she thought it was a riot that this other woman had paid for her face-lift with her MasterCard. I couldn't see why that was funny. To be honest, I thought it was pretty damn impressive. If I tried to raise my *eyebrow* using my MasterCard, it would be instantly declined. I would *love* to have enough funds in any credit card to allow me to hand it to a plastic surgeon without the fear that he would break the card over his knee the way the army breaks your sword when you're court-martialled.

When I had finished Rita Mae's wonderful book, there was nothing else to read on the flight except the local daily paper. I usually grab this just when they announce that landing is happening pretty soon, not least because of the trend for pilots to announce that they're going to land "in the Detroit area" or "the Atlanta area". Scares the shit out of me, that vagueness. I always figure the plane's going to come down in a suburban back yard or swimming pool rather than the airport. To keep my mind off the options the pilot might prefer to the actual airport, during this last fifteen minutes of the flight I go through the local paper. On this occasion, a blocked-out ad on page 5 leaped out at me.

"New Advances in Plastic Surgery", it said, a picture of a surgeon beside the headline. Lecture, it said, on Tuesday. At lunchtime. In the HQ of Associates in Cosmetic Surgery. Free. Seating limited, so please call in advance and make your reservation. The guy in the picture was Dr Brueck.

My diary said I could be at the lecture without hassle. The day after my arrival, I telephoned to reserve a seat.

"Date of birth?" the telephonist asked.

Lady, when I reserve a seat in a theatre, I don't usually get asked my date of birth, I thought.

"Why do you need my date of birth?"

"It's standard," she said, sounding suddenly unsure.

"Why?"

"I have to put you on hold for just a moment," she said, and catapulted me into a recording. Not of music. This recording was a golden syrup man's voice.

"Dr Brueck also presents the Obagi skin repair system," he told me. "Obagi products restore and regulate normal skin functions, so that your skin can function as a natural barrier against the harmful elements in nature ..."

What the hell, I wondered, were these "normal skin functions" that had to be restored and regulated? Skin was for holding you together and keeping the wet out. Other than those functions, it doesn't do anything else particularly well. When you're pregnant, there isn't enough of it, so it has to be stretched a bit, and you end up after the baby is born with marks to remind you of the stretching. They look as if a snail had visited you. When you're forty, you have too much skin, so you have to sellotape it behind your ears. But whether you're pregnant or unpregnant, young or old, the skin *always* can "function as a natural barrier against the harmful elements in nature", so what gives with this claim? Have you managed to help skin resist the effects of radiation or what? Otherwise, I –

"Gloria here, how may I help you?"

Different voice, same routine. The age detective had obviously abandoned me and run away. I let this new telephonist go through the routine and when she got to the date of birth, gave her Hitler's.

For a moment, she came close to telling me I sounded very young for someone that old, but she restrained herself and said my place was reserved and they looked forward to seeing me on Tuesday.

On Tuesday, the venue turned out to be a small office block, and the lecture happened in a converted office. A luxurious converted office, but a converted office, nonetheless, its main desk shunted over to one side and covered with a tablecloth. On top were coffee, tea, soft drinks and sandwiches. Packed into the room were thirty chairs. Twenty-seven women, three men. Twenty women in their sixties or older. Ten in the fifty-plus region. I was the youngest there, Hitler's birthdate notwithstanding.

As they gathered coffees and drinks, I watched them. Some had clearly come in twos for moral support. The singletons circled the others, pretending not to do what of course they were doing: working out how badly the other person needed plastic surgery. Since we were in the Deep South, they were all mahogany-coloured, except for the really old ones, who had that talcum-powdery whiteness laced with grey liver spots.

The room was awash in coping behaviours. Several of the women had those ash-blonde page-boy hairdos that cover up the forehead and conceal as much as possible of the cheeks and neck.

One, near me, had an agonized series of poses, all designed to keep her chin up and her ears back so as to minimize the wrinkles scoring her face. When she sat down, one hand went to her jaw, an index finger extended to conceal where the skin was sagging away from the bone.

Another woman, a scarf knotted around her neck, was so carefully made up that when she put her hand to her face, it looked as if it belonged to a different person – un-made-up, knotty at the joins and thinly covered in sheeny crinkled old-lady skin of such delicacy you feared it might rub off. Several of the women and one of the men had the physique and the clothes of constant tennis players.

Each of us pretended we were simply there to learn about the concept of plastic surgery. Just to keep up to date with an important aspect of medicine, don't you know. A woman in her thirties in a white coat and carrying a clipboard welcomed us and took us through Dr Brueck's qualifications. He was a Licentiate of this and a Board member of that. This man was covered, head to toe, in qualifications. You wondered how he ever got time to eat, but when he stood up, you knew he found the time. Dr Brueck is a big lump of good-looking, middle-aged charm. Up behind him pops a list of what he's going to deal with. Chemical peels. Laser peels. Eyelid surgery. Lip enhancement. Face-lifts. Brow-lifts.

He's halfway into skin peels before I work out how face-lifts and brow-lifts differ. I had always assumed face-lifts were an all-over job, but in fact they're south-of-the-border operations: below the eyes, affecting the chin, cheeks and neck, but ignoring the forehead.

The pictures he shows are fascinating, starting with the shots of patients after they have had a chemical skin peel. They all seem to develop a shiny smoothness that reminds me of the aftermath of a vicious sunburn, when your blistered skin has come off in long shards. It looks shiny and taut, like a convalescent rather than a healthy person's natural smoothness. Thumbs down to chemical peels. Anyway, the recovery time could suit only a retired person.

It's perfectly clear that Brueck himself is bored stupid by chemical peels, because he lashes along through that section. He comes alive when he gets to laser resurfacing. His listeners get the message: this is the new, improved version of the peel.

The laser he uses, he says, sends a spurt of light that evaporates the top layer of skin. Whiff. Just like that. Gone. The surgeon can take the equivalent of a damp dishcloth and just wipe away the ashes of the outer skin. The next layer of skin seems to get scared, finding its outer clothing gone missing, and contracts in terror. So when it heals, the skin that's left, the skin that's revealed by the killing off of the top layer, is smooth and tight and – for some reason he doesn't bother to explain – thicker than it was beforehand.

"This young lady", Brueck says, producing a slide of a woman in her mid-sixties, "had spent a lot of time out of doors and as a result had extensive sun damage and wrinkling. We did a laser resurfacing and –"

Sound of standing ovulation. Hisses of indrawn breath. The withered old lady who had been so wrinkled that her wrinkles almost overlapped, like little waves catching up with each other at the seashore, beams out at us, smooth and glowing. The old sub-editor in me instantly comes up with a caption: "Complexion goes from Elephant to Apple."

The plastic surgeon, reinforced by the reaction, swells visibly. The lasering, he explains, gets done in little postage-stamp squares. A relief, this, to those of us who were wondering how bad the damage could be if the surgeon got a bit broad-brush about the whole thing. No, he does a postage stamp, checks it, wipes off the dead stuff, then does another postage stamp. The owner of the face being done is in "twilight sleep". Someone behind me opines that this is just as well, because it would hurt like hell if you were awake, plus the smell of your own burning skin might not be a great sensual experience.

Between the before-and-after shots of "this young lady", he now shows us shots of her three days after surgery. So many indrawn breaths are drawn that I'm afraid that, like a cartoon character, I am going to get sucked down someone's throat. Understandable, this in-drawing. The woman is covered in a crusting weepy horror. She is crème brûlée, coated in excrescences of hardened roasted sugar.

Brueck uses our shudders as a platform to lecture us about hygiene. Post-laser, it seems, the patient must wash all this crusted stuff off every hour or so, because if the crust is allowed to settle in, it becomes a breeding ground for bacteria, infection and permanent scarring. He skims over the discomfort involved with a classic medical observation about "any pain is controlled by prescribed analgesia".

As long as six months after the procedure, Brueck adds, the skin is reddish, but corrective make-up takes care of that. Our aestheticians, Barbara and JoAnn, will tell us all about the techniques a little later.

Eyelid surgery and lip enhancement don't get anything like the response the group gave to laser resurfacing. Partly because the eyelids he shows us are so grotesquely over-hung with spare skin, none of us relate to their owners. The patients look awake and rested after the surgery, having looked hungover, depressed, half-asleep and tortoise-like beforehand.

Lip enhancement sounds iffy. Fat can be withdrawn from somewhere else in the body and injected into the lips, but it doesn't seem to hang around there a long time, and who wants to spend the rest of their life having syringes stuck in their bottoms to "harvest" fat to inject in their lips? An alternative is to have a textile called Gore-Tex threaded through the lips, which fattens up the outer rim enough to prevent those nasty puckers developing.

You get the impression, as you listen, that all these methods of reducing or preventing draw-string mouth are not a patch on what's coming up in Brueck's lecture: that there is some overall procedure that will take care of the puckers and a bunch of other problems, simultaneously. Face-lift, you think. Definitely face-lift.

"Now, to face-lifts," he says and the people in his audience nod wisely to one another.

He shows us a picture of another "young lady" in her sixties on whom he has done a face-lift. The audience is now perilously close to a bunch of religious groupies undertaking ecstasy. Show 'em a before-and-after and it's orgasms all round. Never mind that the Before shots always seem to have been taken when the patient was garbed in bag-lady chic, half dead from the cold and suffering from self-esteem so low it could slide under a door. The After shots always show the same person made up to the nines, dressed to the gills, freshly coiffed and beaming like a lottery winner. Their attitude is obviously so far removed from their mood in the first photograph that even if a scalpel had never gone near them, they would seem vastly improved.

At this stage, Brueck points out that this woman did not have a brow-lift, and we all agree that, yes, she does still have a few lines up there under the bangs. But because the rest of her face is so improved, none of us had noticed them. The doctor makes the point that you can get away with having one of the procedures, preferably the face-lift, and leave the other part of your face alone. Of course, you can always have both together, but he doesn't advise it.

Why not? Because if you get a face-lift – a good face-lift – you will look great, but nobody will immediately work out why, whereas if you have the two together, the improvement is so radical, your appearance will scream "Plastic surgery!"

Warming to his theme of "The Good Face-lift", Brueck claims that the standard reaction to such a face-lift, when its owner takes it to work, is that colleagues tell you how rested you look, but no more than that. A bad face-lift gives you the wind tunnel look. And a brow-lift done at the same time as a face-lift tends to improve you so radically even the best vacation will not explain it away. He winds up on face-lifts with a random set of shots, makes passing reference to arm-lifts (memo to self: find out about arm-lifts) and asks for questions.

Costs come up first. Chemical peels start at $1,275. Laser resurfacing around the same. Eyelids go for $750–1,300. Lips can get fattened or threaded for as little as $250. (None of these costs, he adds, include the surgery-room charges. Essentially, what he's giving us are his personal fees. Extra money has to go for the rent of the hall.) Face-lifts start at $2,900.

How long do they last? Laser resurfacing longer than chemical peels, that's for sure. Face-lifts? The first lasts three to four years, but successive ones last as long as ten. He advances no reasons for why it lasts longer on a second or third go.

How old or young should you be? He has done face-lifts, he says, on women in their thirties, and also on one woman in her eighties. No problems with either end of the age scale.

How exactly is a face-lift done? He loves this question. Loves it as much as the audience hate the answer.

We learn, for the first time, that the knife goes in at the ear, trails down at the hairline to the neck, and that after that first incision, the next step is to slice the skin loose from the underlying facial structures, practically as far in as the nose. I must be imagining things, I think. He can't be telling me that halfway through this surgery, your facial skin is anchored only by a narrow panel down the middle of your face and that if they sat you up and put a high wind behind your head, you could end up with two great flaps of skin like wings, tethered by your nose.

Getting dizzy from the awfulness of it, I put my head as near to my knees as I can so as not to faint. In that position, I find myself automatically patting my cheeks as if to say "Don't worry. Wouldn't ever do such a nasty to you."

Meanwhile, the man I'm temporarily calling Brueck the Butcher goes on, happily, describing how he drags the skin taut (like Saran-wrap), stitches it in place and cuts off the extra. Or maybe cuts off the extra and then stitches it in place. I can't concentrate on the sequence. When he begins to talk about doing the same sort of thing north of the nose in a brow-lift, I stuff my fingers in my ears and sing songs to myself.

The next time I plug in to what he is saying, he is giving a ritual warning that nobody should think face-lifts turn back the clock. Unexpectedly, I hear a dissident male somewhere behind me muttering that he can't understand why the surgeon is makin' such a dang fuss 'bout not turnin' back the clock. Looks to him, the unseen male says, *sotto voce*, that the before-and-after shots explicitly indicate that turnin' back the clock is *precisely* what a face-lift does.

I would love to have a chat with my unseen friend, because the more I look, the more correct I think the surgeon is. Face-lifts don't make people look younger. They just make them look good. Just as removing huge jangly earrings or spectacles with rhinestones in the frames takes away a distraction, removing redundant skin does away with a face-full of distracting wrinkles, so you can see what someone really looks like. In much the same way, those close-up photographs of the Sistine Chapel do Michelangelo a disservice. The viewer spends time noticing the cobweb of interlaced cracks in the paint, as opposed to registering the beauty of the overall composition.

Nonetheless, I do not wish to seem like an easy touch for the plastic surgery message. Let's get a bit of tough reality into this, I think, and raise my hand. Brueck nods, welcomingly.

"Two questions. Firstly, how many face-lifts have you done? Secondly, what was the worst result you had?"

I can feel the audience's hatred: little laser postage stamps all over me from their horrified gaze. These clearly are unacceptable questions. Not, however, to Dr Brueck, who says he's done in excess of a thousand face-lifts.

"I remember when I was first asked that question about a particular procedure," he says, in high good humour. "I was at the very start of my career, and I'm standing in a hospital corridor with a potential patient and she asks me how many of the procedures I've done. And at that point, I've done all of four of them. This is what I tell her, and I do not think the number greatly increases her belief that I should undertake the surgery with her. I was not aware until later that the conversation had been overheard by my mentor, a much older plastic surgeon, who later that day called me to one side and said, 'Robert, if someone ever asks you how many times you have undertaken a procedure, here is what you do. You put your hand to your forehead and you look up to the sky as if you were searching your memory for the past forty years, and you say How many have I done? Hmm ... and by that stage they will have decided you have done 4,000 of them and will leave you alone.'"

The audience laughs. Dr Brueck smiles his way through the laughter, but his eyes reflect the fact that he is already processing the second question.

"The worst outcome I ever had? That's easy. Easy because it was so horrific, it is etched in my memory forever."

Hush descends.

"It must be eighteen years ago."

Clever, I think. Anything bad that ever happened to you happened in pre-history.

"The patient was in her early fifties, and the surgery – a face-lift – went without a hitch. The next day I was going around the hospital (at that time face-lifts were procedures demanding a week-long stay in hospital), and when I knocked and entered her room, her back was to me and her husband was seated, facing me from the opposite side of her bed. I came into the room in a very upbeat frame of mind, because the surgery had gone well, but I was halted by the expression of absolute fear and horror on her husband's face. 'Is this what's supposed to happen?' he asked. 'Is this normal?' With that, his wife turned to face me and the sight of her almost brought me to my knees."

The air in the room has turned clammy as he pauses before the next bit of the story.

"Swelling is considerable after facial surgery of this kind, so I expected swelling and discoloration," he goes on. "But what I had not expected to see was an open suppurating wound – an almost continuous open wound. Her skin was sloughing away from the stitches. It was frankly difficult not to show my horror, but I managed to remain superficially calm and to say that complications of this kind were not unknown and would require immediate decisive intervention. I had her back in the operating theatre within an hour and a team of us worked as we had never worked before – and as I have never worked since that day. We could not, at that time, bring the procedure to the ideal level, but we could halt the sloughing and ensure she would not be disfigured for life. I hope never to encounter anything like it again. The second surgery worked, and about a year later we went back to get her appearance to what we should have been able to expect after the first surgery."

I look around at the audience. The woman who had earlier lined up her index finger with her sagging jawline is now chewing lumps out of the index finger. It is left to one of the men to ask the key question.

"Why did it happen?"

For the first time, Brueck moves from charming salesman to no-messing medic.

"Smoking."

"Smoking?"

"The patient was a heavy smoker, although she had not admitted this prior to the surgery. Smoking robs the tissues of the nutrients and minerals needed for healing. It decreases blood supply and oxygen to the tissues. It measurably increases the risk of post-operative infection. Since that experience, I have made it a policy never to operate on a heavy smoker. If you are a heavy smoker, you will give up cigarettes for eight weeks before the surgery, and we will test every week to validate what you tell us. You will not smoke for eight weeks after surgery, either. It is just too dangerous."

Everybody wants to change the subject, but nobody wants to ask another question. Not publicly, anyway. I suspect several of them want to have quiet little chats with the charming surgeon, but not to voice their concerns aloud. So he gestures at the sandwiches and indicates that the "aestheticians" will now move in, to talk about how wearing green make-up conceals the redness resulting from laser resurfacing.

I grab a folder of information and leave. It has been interesting. In a general way, of course. Not a personal way. I'm still categorizing myself as "not the face-lift type", although now that I can feel the wobbling of my wattles without even applying a finger to them, I am less cocksure about life membership of that category.

However, there are other considerations to take into account. One of them I am married to, and if I think *I'm* not the face-lift type, Tom is very definitely not the face-lift type, nor the married-to-a-face-lift type.

The other consideration is money. Not only will my credit card not go near something as costly as this, but my bank account has been eaten away – pardon the expression – by the first instalment on the teeth implants.

So face-lifts are not, I tell myself in a disciplined way, a real possibility within the next ten years.

Later, they may come into play. Much later. Maybe.

6

The lure of lipo

A few months after that, I paid another visit to my motor-mechanic dental surgeon, who uncovered the posts deep in my gums and screwed temporary top things to them. The purpose of these is to get the gums used to having things not made of bone protruding through them, and also to allow impressions to be made for the permanent superstructure that is to be screwed onto these posts in due course.

Everything is doing well, I am assured. When I stop at the little glass booth within his office where his administrative staff are stationed, I find them giggling over something onscreen. One of them, slightly shamefacedly, tells me they've come across an Internet site completely devoted to the fact that Hillary Clinton has thick ankles. I suggest that this is one of the few things over which neither Mrs Clinton nor anyone else has control. Mrs Clinton could lose all the weight in the world, but still end up with thick ankles, it being a genetic, rather than an obesity, problem.

"Not at all," one of the nurses says briskly. "She should have liposuction. Perfect for cases like that."

The other nurse does an eyes-to-heaven expression and murmurs that this new nurse hasn't shaken off the bad habit of plugging her previous employer, a plastic surgery place that advertises in the newspapers.

She mentions advertising in newspapers as if it were a practice roughly equal to child molesting. The other nurse laughs as she shrugs on her coat.

"That's where the nursing jobs of the future will be," she promises. "You mark my words. They're so busy over there, they practically have to have their surgeons like pilots – only working so many hours, in case they get too tired to do it properly."

The nurse and I walk out together. I ask her why she left the plastic surgery clinic.

"Lack of variety," she says. "I assisted the surgeon who does the lipo, and it's very successful and all that, but after a while it gets a bit boring. I mean, the patient's unconscious and the doctor is just rooting around under their skin for the fat, and what's to do except monitor their vital signs?"

I ask how much weight can be removed at any one time. She shakes her head as we get into the elevator. That's not the way it's done, she says; it's not really a method of solving obesity.

"The clinic where I worked, they had a ban on ever taking out more than ten pounds, no matter what the patient weighed, and if the patient wasn't heavy to start with, the surgeon might not take any more than a pound. Otherwise you'd have patients going into shock, you know? Most of the time, the surgeon is getting the fat out of some area on the patient's body where no amount of dieting or exercise will do it, so it's not weight that is the issue, really. If you've got fat knees or fat ankles, it might only be a few pounds that's creating the fat appearance, but if you can get rid of those few pounds, you just feel great."

But what, I ask, happens when the fat comes back. It doesn't, she maintains. The body has only so many fat cells and if you remove it surgically, you remove it for all time. There's nothing to stop the patient getting very overweight at some later date, but the overwhelming bulk of the extra fat will go somewhere else on the body, not to wherever the liposuction was done.

I wonder aloud, as we walk to our cars, about socialites having lipo to allow them to fit into a tight dress that night. She shakes her head and explains that when the fat gets taken out, the surgeon fills – even overfills – the vacuum created by injecting it with antibiotic in a sort of gel, so the patient goes out sloshily heavier than when she arrived. This extra freight gets absorbed by the body over a few weeks, during which the patient must wear special pressure undergarments, because otherwise the body would not shrink evenly, and who wants big irregular dimples?

Nobody wants big irregular dimples, I agree, and tell her I'll see her when I come back, six weeks thereafter, to have the first fitting of what I hope will be teeth for life.

There is no rhyme or reason to the fact that the minute I get back to the office, I telephone the clinic and ask for liposuction immediately if not sooner. They make noises about preliminary visits and waiting lists, and I get terse and demanding. I find myself talking to a woman called Dexy. She does a ritual dance with me on the phone, to check out what kind of lunatic is suddenly possessed by the notion that liposuction will solve all her life's problems.

"I am very realistic, Dexy," I say firmly. "I know liposuction is not a solution to obesity, but I am not obese. I simply have a spare tyre and a protruding stomach and all my winter clothes are tight-fitting."

This, peculiarly, seems to convince her that I am not a psychological stray attributing more to lipo than it can deliver, and she becomes quite enthusiastic, telling me that this clinic specializes in the most modern form of lipo. Apparently, in the bad old days (two or three years ago) surgeons stuck their tubes into bodies, rooted around and sucked out whatever fat they could find, brutally.

Today, however, they first of all inject this preliminary material to make the fat tumescent, then introduce cannulas of varying size beneath the skin.

"What's a cannula?" I ask, although I really do not want to know.

A tube, she says. I imagine a blunt-ended tube being rammed into my skin. I block out the thought. Even a syringe going into my skin has always been a major challenge to me, so a tube gives me the screaming meemies.

"... and because he uses only syringes and very delicate tubing in the superficial fat directly under the skin," Dexy is going on, "there are never dinges or dents or runnels in the skin to serve as a giveaway."

I agree that runnels in the skin are not acceptable under any circumstances. She is on a roll at this point, wanting to tell me precisely how marvellous their surgeon is. A sculptor in flesh, she says. For a moment, I think she is being ironic, and then realize that no, this lady seriously believes her surgeon is a Michelangelo: the Leonardo of Lipo. I figure that jeering at this concept will not get me seen quickly, and so I encourage her to expand on the theme. By the time she's ground to a halt, the only question in any listener's mind has to be how on earth this man has not exhibited his work at the Met.

"Don't you ever have cancellations?" I ask, wondering what the hell is wrong with me that I am asking, in effect, to be put on a standby list for tubes to be rammed into my person to remove bulges that are bothering nobody but me, and not even me all that much.

Occasionally, she admits, they do have cancellations, but it's very rare. And it's never any good to another patient. Why not? Because, she says, the only reason anybody would ever cancel an appointment with Leonardo is if they have a cold, because of course he could not proceed in the presence of an infection. But this in turn means that the notice is usually very short. A woman telephoned this morning, she explains, who has flu, and who therefore can't be lipo-ed tomorrow at the appointed time of 12.15, but no other patient could take up an appointment at such short notice.

"I could," I hear myself say.

"But you're not a patient."

"If he does lipo on me tomorrow, I'd be a patient."

"There has to be a preliminary examination."

"Fine."

"But that would have to take place before the surgery."

"Obviously."

"No, I mean before he does any surgery on anybody tomorrow."

"So what time does he start?"

She begins to laugh and indicates that the pre-operative behaviour of most patients is quite unlike mine. Most patients, she explains, need lots of time to think about it. They need counselling to make sure they have no unreasonable expectations. How can they be sure I have no unreasonable expectations? I point out that I have no expectations at all.

"Then why do you want it done and done so suddenly?" she asks, reasonably enough.

"Because when I'm buying anything, I can't bear any delays. I just want it now."

"But this isn't really buying something," she says in a puritanical voice.

"You giving it away?"

She laughs again and remarks that I don't seem to be of a nervous or troubled disposition, and that maybe we could look at the possibility. Could I be there at 10.30? I would have to stay from that point until it was time to move into the operating theatre, and I'd have to starve from midnight, not even a glass of water to pass my lips. We do a deal on the phone. I will get stomach, spare tyre and top of thighs done for a knock-down fee of £1,500. Normally, she promises me, it would cost more, but since I am actually doing them a slight favour in taking up the space left by the woman with the flu, they will acknowledge that in the cost to me. I am to wear a tracksuit. Mmm, I say, never in my life having owned a tracksuit or anything like it. She reminds me about the starving from midnight and we part company.

I don't even tell Tom about the conversation and the plan, because – well, why? If I go to work in the morning, neither he nor anyone else need ever know.

This is not like the implants, where I have to go to hospital for a couple of days for some of the stages of the process. This is simple. Small-time. Minor corrective work. Not worth wasting his time on. And anyway, having booked myself on impulse for a costly procedure about which I have severe reservations, I can't face Tom's disbelieving, puzzled questioning. What he doesn't know won't hurt me, I think.

So, the following day, I wear one of my multi-layered outfits to the office. Long loose skirt, topped by a loose tunic-type top, topped by a long, light duster coat. One of the girls says it makes me look like a wandering nomad eating nothing but yogurt and singing to camels. Because of having to starve, I hate her for the reference to delicious yogurt.

Just after ten, I announce that I have to go and buy something and I have no idea if I will be back. It is a very important secret purchase, I announce, and I'm telling nobody about it, and they can expect me when they see me. But I am, of course, reachable on my mobile phone. I then "accidentally" ensure that it is left on the windowsill in my office, switched on, so that someone will be attracted to its ringing and not get worried about it being switched off. Any fool can leave their cellphone behind them.

Sans mobile phone, I arrive at the clinic at the appointed time and meet Dexy, who is – she says – a grandmother, but doesn't look it. She takes me in to meet Leonardo the Laconic. He is in surgical greens and clogs with a mask hanging on his chest. He gestures at a chair and goes through a form to find my basic soundness level in wind and limb. He then does a brief physical examination.

"What's this?" he says, pointing to brown marks on the inside

[85]

of my fingers. For a moment, I don't identify what the stain is, then realize, and tell him, that it comes from applying instant tan without first putting on gloves or scrubbing the hands at length directly afterwards.

"Not smoking, then?"

"I've never smoked," I say coolly.

He invites me to hike up my tunic, lower my skirt and show him the problem. I do. He takes a permanent marker in hand and does concentric circles on my skin with it, as if he was drawing a cross-section of a tree. When I have concentric circles on lower chest, stomach and top of thighs, he then puts me against the wall and takes pictures of his drawings, "for comparison purposes", he says. I am tempted to ask who's going to be compared with me.

He approaches me with a pre-operative injection, which he says is Valium. This puzzles me. Why would I need a tranquillizer if I am not anxious? I decide not to make an issue of it, however, figuring that since he was supposed to start operating fifteen minutes ago, I should let him get on with it, or he will not get to me at all.

I am taken away from his room, changed into one of those dreadful gowns that ties down the back, given a towelling dressing gown and put in a cubicle where I have the choice of getting into a bed or sitting on a bentwood chair. I turn on my laptop, put it on the bed, sit in the chair and have lots of work done before they arrive for me.

I walk into the operating theatre, which seems awfully casual compared to any operating theatre I have ever been in before, but they explain that the incisions are very small and so it is not like open-heart surgery. One of the nurses gets an I/V into my arm and tells me that I will be sort of conscious when the doctor is doing his thing, and I can indicate any discomfort at any stage. She does not say what the response to such an indication will be, but I assume they will either pump me fuller of anaesthetic or he will go easier with the tubes.

Leonardo arrives, soft-footed in his surgical clogs, and puts me lying face down. With surprising speed, he does something to the I/V that makes me drift within seconds. He hauls up the robe at the back, revealing his circles. I must, I think, look like a series of bull's-eye dartboards. I can feel needles going into various parts of my anatomy as the nurse tells me this is to numb the skin before the cannulas are inserted. A couple of minutes later, there is a thumping sensation and something enters deep into my thigh. I gasp in astonishment at the alien sensation.

"What? Pain?" Leonardo asks.

He has to be the most economical user of words I've come across. Confused and a little fuzzy, I admit it was shock, rather than pain. There is a moment or two before I feel anything else, and just as I begin to notice the tube moving about from side to side, the sense of drift intensifies, and I am no longer in control of what is going on. No longer do I have even the illusion of control. I am in a dream of tubes and being turned over and occasional discomforts that draw deep moans from me and result in more drift and the next thing I know Leonardo has gone away and the nurses are helping me into an extraordinary white elasticated thing which is a cross between a corset and a bandage.

Then I am in the bed on which I had laid the laptop, and the choice is tea and toast or coffee and sandwiches.

"No variations allowed?" I ask. "You don't permit coffee and toast or tea and sandwiches?"

One of the nurses laughs and says I am recovering too damn quickly and will want out of there soon. I do not tell her that I have already looked at my watch and learned that it is almost one o'clock and that I stand a very good chance of making it back to the office after lunchtime.

Coffee and toast arrive and I drink about two pints of the strong coffee, black. Now fully awake, I begin to check how I feel.

Achey, is the immediate answer. My thighs are settling in for a session of resentful stiffness, while my stomach area feels much the same way as it might during a bad set of menstrual cramps. They offer paracetamol or something stronger. I opt for the paracetamol. When they draw the curtains around the bed, I get out of it and begin to get dressed. One of the nurses, coming back for the tray, looks startled to find me slipping on the duster coat.

"What are you doing?"

"Getting dressed."

"Why?"

"The folks at work might be a little perturbed if I were to arrive at my office wearing nothing but a perfectly clean pressure bandage."

"You're not going back to work."

"Of course I'm going back to work."

"Wait."

I wait. Several nurses and Dexy arrive, to tell me nobody ever goes back to work directly after liposuction, what is wrong with me? Patients like to go home and rest. It's Friday afternoon. My business can manage without me for an afternoon.

"My business can manage without me for much more than an afternoon," I agree. "But what's the problem? I feel wonderful,

I've been walking around here for the last half hour. If I get tired or anything back at the office, they'll take care of me, whereas if I go home, I go home to an empty house, which is not half as safe."

They eventually cave in, and one of them is deputed to take care of me. But because she is due to have lunch, she hands me over, when it comes to going to the reception area, to a tea-lady who happens to be heading in that direction. The tea-lady presents me to the receptionist and asks her to call me a taxi.

I tell the receptionist I don't actually need a taxi, that my car is parked outside. The receptionist doesn't give a sugar one way or the other, and has no notion that I probably should not be allowed to drive after what I have been through, because she doesn't know, does she, what precisely I have been through, down that long corridor? So out the door I go, into my car and back to work.

At work, nobody notices my being thinner, mainly because I am not. Underneath the loose-layered outfit, the pressure bandage consolidates the flesh that has had antibiotic liquid injected into it to such an extent that it feels swollen, loose, liquid and floppy. They have warned me about leakage and padded me around with plastic sheeting with absorbent tissue on one side. I check for and find a little leakage at the top of my right thigh, but otherwise, I am, if not watertight, at least antibiotic-tight. I get through the afternoon's work and am home long before Tom arrives. Which means I can re-bandage and examine myself in the long mirror.

The mirror and scales indicate that I am about twelve pounds heavier than I was this morning. This guy does not economize on antibiotic liquid, that's for sure. Some of the points where the cannulas went in are leaking softly. I press the softly padded flesh on either side of the puncture mark and find that I can create a little fountain. I enjoy this so much that instead of fixing something for me and Tom to eat, I keep at it until I realize I may be endangering the protection provided by the antibiotic. Once that realization sinks home, I velcro myself back into the bandage/corset and get on with the evening. I feel slightly stuffed and liquidy – a human waterbed – but otherwise have neither symptoms nor problems.

It takes about six weeks for all the antibiotic to be absorbed and for it to be safe to take off the bandage/corset. I get the impression from the literature the clinic provides that if you do not wear the corset thing all day, every day, your skin will lose its affection for its understructure and never stick properly to it again. I do not want my skin to develop this detached attitude, so I wear the garment. They have given me three replacements, so laundering is not a problem. The nearest thing to a problem is the fact that, at night, it tends to roll down at the top, leaving the torso bit exposed. I find myself getting up several times a night to roll it back up. Tom wakes every time.

"What the hell are you at?" he asks, in the dark.

"You don't want to know," I tell him.

When eventually I have healed, washed all the indelible marker away, and abandoned the bandage, I am very satisfied with the result of the liposuction. I am also pretty bloody annoyed over all the years I spent doing sit-ups in order to flatten my stomach. The surgery has done it better – and, if they are to be believed, a hell of a lot more permanently, and with a great deal more ease and comfort. Of course, sit-ups don't cost £1,500, but on the other hand, time taken in sit-ups could probably have been devoted with much profit to some other activity.

I can now wear ribbed snug-fitting sweaters, because I have no longer got that soft roundness under my bustline. I can also wear tight skirts made of lycra without a convexity at the front – my hipbones have a flatness between them. An area of bulge which used to show up in leggings, not that I plan to spend a lot of time in leggings, has been removed from the top of each thigh, so the line of my upper leg is much more straight and pleasing. I would even say "sculpted", but I would not want to buy in to Dexy's portrayal of Leonardo.

The two of them appeared on television about two months after I had the liposuction. Some singing star in her early twenties had been selected by a television programme to undergo a major make-over, including radical reshaping by liposuction, and the clinic where I had been for my few hours had agreed to do it, I assume free of charge, for the publicity.

The general reaction of the people in the office who saw the second of the two programmes devoted to the make-over was that liposuction, as demonstrated, was a snare and a delusion. Cameras had gone in and watched the process, right down to the putting of plastic bottles of yellow human fat outside the back door of the clinic for pick up by waste contractors. This latter image was the one which made several of the men in the office gag. One of the older guys described lipo as the twentieth century's high-tech version of the vomitorium, which passed (mercifully) over the heads of most of the people who heard the comment.

"She isn't thinner," one of them said. "Did you notice, they didn't even weigh her, and they had planned to? I bet you she started to pig out the minute she'd had the lipo and they were too embarrassed to admit you could gain back the fat in so little time."

The girl certainly looked tubbier after the surgery than one had expected. But the authorities I had read all said that while someone might well gain back weight if they chose to eat like hell in the aftermath of the surgery, they would become fatter within the improved shape dictated by the lipo. You could, in other words, become an hour and a half within an hourglass shape. Which, the experts pointed out, was still a hell of an improvement over, for example, a basic barrel-of-lard shape.

For me, the experiment was a success. A speedy, painless and relatively inexpensive success.

COST: Half a day, £1,500
VERDICT: 9 out of 10 (and I might have it done to some other part)

Not long afterwards, I had the final fitting for the bottom teeth implants. A horseshoe-shaped set of teeth was affixed permanently to the posts sticking up from my jaw, and after a week or so of unease, I quickly got used to the sensation of absolute sure solidity. I could chew as if these were my real, natural teeth. Indeed, I could chew better and more confidently than when I had owned my real, natural teeth.

These teeth stood up a little from the gum to allow one to clean between the posts with a special toothbrush that looked like a little broomstick. When, six weeks after they were put in place, I went back to the dentist for a final examination, I told him I was so happy with them I was now going to save for the same thing to be done on my upper jaw.

He said, cautiously, that upper jaws were more complicated than lower jaws and I should not expect so straightforward an experience if I decided to go that road, although his patient Mrs Dolan now had upper and lowers and had sent her regards to me. I gazed at him, trying to figure out who Mrs Dolan was. Eventually it clicked. The little housewife who had mortgaged her home to pay for dental implants and got her sex life back as a result. I asked him to give her my love and told him I'd see him next year.

That £25,000 was a fair price, I felt, if only for the comfort of knowing that, over the coming twenty years, if I should live that long, my face will not collapse, because the bone of my lower jaw has erosion-protection built in. But it is also very pleasant to go back to the experience of youth, when one had a full lower set of real teeth ready to bite into anything. When I mention this to the surgeon, he says he believes research is going to show that people with implants will live a lot longer than people with false teeth.

This floors me, and he explains that research already shows that having false teeth shortens one's lifespan. On average, of course. Each of us knows a ninety-five-year-old thriving away despite not having had a tooth of her own since her twenties. Notwithstanding healthy exceptions, the reality is that because false teeth are intrinsically so unsatisfactory and limiting, their users tend to restrict their own diets, so that, absent fresh or raw vegetables and fruits, absent the occasional good steak, they become malnourished and less resistant to infection. Ergo, he concludes, he expects implants to considerably extend the lifespan of those who lose their natural teeth.

It will take time, of course, for research to prove his personal thesis, but I am prepared, for obvious reasons, to believe it straight away, since it suggests that not only will my face not collapse, but I might survive a little longer because of titanium implants in my jaw.

Admittedly, even though I know that this is the end of only the first instalment of completely artificial permanent teeth, I can answer an enthusiastic affirmative to the question: Am I glad I did it?

Couldn't be gladder, in fact. There is no downside, other than the tedium and length of the process, to implanted teeth.

COST: Six days over two years, £25,000
VERDICT: 10 out of 10

7

Older means invisible

For a few months, the results of the liposuction and the implanted teeth kept me relatively happy. Any time the thought of a face-lift came to mind, I told myself that someone like me could not really fall for what has to be the quintessential self-indulgence, demonstrating the superficiality of the owner of the face.

"People of character, wisdom and intellect age gracefully," I would tell myself. "There is a great beauty in the unadorned older face of a woman who has truly lived. It is not the banal prettiness of youth, but a much more profound loveliness informed by time, by suffering, by joy and by pain ..."

"Oh yeah?" a lawless little voice would question, inside my head. "Show me."

Watching the world around me, I found that difficult. First of all, relatively few women age well. A woman can work out, take care of her grooming, de-tox twice a year at a spa and still look ropey in her fifties and sixties, whereas many men who take damn-all exercise, eat the wrong foods and drink hard liquor by the barrel end up looking ambassadorial at the same age. Which proves nothing other than that there's no justice in matters of gender.

Even when I would spot an older woman who did have an unadorned serene beauty to her face, I rarely saw it surrounded by hushed admiration. *Au contraire.* In the office, when a famous female over fifty appeared on the television set we keep in the corner, you could be sure someone, attracted by the familiar face on screen, would say "Gawd, she's looking very old, isn't she?"

I kept listening out for comments like "See the wisdom in that woman's face, see how beautiful her eyes are, doesn't she look more interesting now than she did at thirty?" They never came, those comments. Not about women. Sometimes about men. Never about women. About women, the comments were about jowliness or deep lines from nose to mouth, or pathetic efforts at age-concealment. ("Who does she think she's kidding, with the scarf casually thrown around the turkey neck? We're on to you, lady ...")

Nor was it simply that the evidence of age was being observed neutrally. There was a heavy, final dismissal in the comments. A condemnation. A deadly verdict often echoed in captions under pictures in newspapers and magazines, its negativity obvious and (presumably) editorially approved.

"The ageing Brigitte Bardot," the caption would run, delivering a sweeping backhand smack.

Not by the wildest stretch of imagination could that "ageing" be considered a positive description. In some other century, maybe, but at a time when sexiness is everything, "ageing" means the opposite, carrying connotations of a flaccid decay and pallid sagginess as repellent as a burglar alarm.

I began to notice other unlikely women on the run. Writers, for God's sake, whose age or appearance shouldn't matter at all, were either trying to confuse the public as to how old they were (Nuala O'Faolain, in the publicity around the launch of her first novel, being imprecise as to where she is in her sixties) or writing grimly about how you become invisible once you hit fifty (Clare Boylan).

The signs of being fifty seemed pretty obvious. I sat one night in my local bar, smiling through a banter session led by men but not excluding women. The subject? Whether a woman's face ages as fast or faster than her cleavage. The men present gave millimetre-precise distinctions between the young cleavage and the old. The unacceptability of the old cleavage was a given, rather than a topic for debate. Nobody in their right minds would find old cleavage attractive. Not only that, but it was The Age Giveaway. No matter how a woman acted, or exercised or dressed, once you saw the cleavage you could tell her age, practically to the year. Like rings in a tree trunk.

Nobody in the pub that night talked about the ineffable beauty of authentic, honest ageing. They talked with clever terrifying casualness about something which self-evidently, to them, removed women from the mainstream into an irrelevant sub-species whose only contribution might be as comedy turns. *Low* comedy turns: the whiskey-voiced old harridan with sprouts of hair erupting on chin and cheek. Older women, ran the subtext, should know their place, and their place is to be invisible.

Knowing myself to be on the cusp of that invisibility (or that low comedy), I stood chilled, vilely tempted by the convivial warmth of collective laughter. I still qualified. I could not just join the jeerers, but better them with jokes about draw-string mouths and puppet wrinkles. ("Puppet wrinkles" are named after those old-fashioned wooden puppets where the lower lip and chin bob up and down independent of the rest of the face.) I could still "pass". I had not yet been disqualified.

In the days following that gleeful night out, I searched for evidence of how we value age. Because we do, don't we? Of course we do. Growing older has always been associated with wisdom, calm – added value. Women like Ninon de l'Enclos had lovers when they were into their nineties because of the delight younger men took in their company.

When I was a teenager, there was a best-selling book by a guy named Stephen Vizinczey, called *In Praise of Older Women*. If I remember his mildly sexploitative thesis, it was that a virile man would probably do better to shag a forty- or fifty-year-old than a teenager or twenty-year-old, because women of advanced years tend to be both experienced and grateful. I presume this book is now out of print, since its thesis is so dated. Dammit, fourteen-year-olds these days are experienced.

Older people are no longer the repository of wisdom. They are no longer the repository of anything younger people need. And that's new. Within living memory, if you wanted to learn particular skills or insights, you learned them from an older person. It was an older woman in the community who passed on the methods for preventing nappy rash in a baby or growing pains in a teenager.

There is no oral culture any more, no continuum of wisdom stored in the heads of ordinary human beings. There has been a general international de-skilling at the hands of "professionals" and as a result of technology.

The professionals have even stolen listening away from the ordinary people. Once upon a time, in misery and terror, humans talked to a friend, a mother, a granny. Now, they pay a total stranger who is a qualified counsellor or therapist. Amateur listening by the old is redundant, and as for the storage of information, wisdom or race-memory, you can buy all that stuff on CD-ROM. You don't want to know how they did something thirty years ago, but even if you did, you can get the data on the Internet, shorn of all the repetitious drivel and tedious personal opinions old farts always insist on including.

Old farts. Wrinklies. Geriatrics. Fogies. They are used, these words, so casually among the young and recently young, they put chills up my spine. Casually used terms so hurtful and destructive that if their equivalents were used about someone's race or gender, it would be actionable. But even sexual harassment has a certain perverse cachet to it that age-contempt lacks. A woman who takes a sexual harassment case against an employer is at least considered attractive enough to harass. But if a woman were to take an age-discrimination case because of being called a "wrinklie", the general reaction would be that, whatever her legal entitlements, the reality is that she is a wrinklie, and it's not very attractive, is it?

When the Equality Authority successfully took Ryanair to court for recruitment ads that indicated they wanted "young, vibrant" staff, some of the best journalists in the country wrote and said that this was political correctness taken to a ludicrous extent. Of *course* companies would want to keep older people out. You wouldn't have a good group dynamic or corporate culture if your staff was made up of the over-forty brigade.

It was like a bizarre replay of the prejudices articulated thirty years earlier when women began to assert themselves. Same daft logic, different angle. Back then, it was that you couldn't let a woman captain a big jet (you'd be taking your life in your hands, she'd be so hysterical coming up to her period) or read the news (nobody'd hear what she was saying, they'd be fancying her so much).

Facts don't get in the way of prejudices involving sex and age. If you've made up your mind that you want only staff under twenty-three years of age, you won't register examples like the American corporation that actively looks to re-hire retirees because it has found them more cost-effective than younger "hires", because they have fewer accidents, fewer sick days, fewer personal problems and demonstrate more loyalty and responsibility. That corporation's sales grew by 20 per cent every year for five years – with an average employee age of seventy-three.

We have no such positive examples in Ireland. Not one. All we have is the law against discrimination and Niall Crowley, over at the Equality Authority, to take action when that law is broken. People are afraid to go to battle on the age issue. In Ireland, there is no "grey power". So, to uninvolved commentators, action on age discrimination is just a funny irritant. To me, as a management consultant, it's more a tragedy. In the past five years, I have witnessed enough real-life case studies to be clear that Ireland is the most unashamedly ageist country in Europe, if not the world.

The case studies turned up in Carr Communications from both the public and the private sector. People from the private sector were coming under benign pressure to take early retirement. Benign as in "Take the good package or be sidelined into Long-

Term Strategic Planning where you can retain a desk and title, plus have the fun of producing documents nobody will ever read."

In the public sector, they came to prepare for promotion interviews, hopelessly convinced that they hadn't a chance, because "they're looking for younger lads, these days".

As the nineties moved on, the resignation in the face of this rampant unacknowledged ageism grew sadder. The women, now in their forties and fifties, who sailed into business and industry as the first fine wave of equal employees, who breached the glass ceilings, now started to walk into glass walls. Here they came, the power-dressed liberated women who featured in the newspaper profiles of their day as First Woman Appointed to Board of ... or Women Joining Ranks of Plumbers / Financial Controllers. Here they came, the women whose potential was initially overestimated because of the need companies had to be able to claim they had a woman in the management team. As tokens, they got so far and thought onward progress inevitable. Now, the conveyor belt had stopped and the rumbles underfoot suggested it would actually reverse.

I remember, as a theatre-struck teenager, hearing an actress in her thirties remarking bitterly that "there's always a younger, prettier version of yourself coming up behind you". In the theatre, that may be an inevitable reality, but until recently, *business-women* did not expect to be fearful of the younger, prettier, better-educated woman behind them. Now, many businesswomen in their forties and fifties are deadly fearful of that woman.

In international fishing they cull baby seals, but in business they cull menopausal women. With just a little less obvious brutality, but great efficiency nonetheless; an efficiency often reinforced by the realism of that first batch of successful women. They know, those women, that their mentors (remember when that was a fashionable concept?) have retired or gone to Head Office. They know that as far as the new CEO is concerned, they are just another old cow down the corridor. They have gone quiet, those once-successful feminists. Quiet, because the vocal weapons that worked so well in the seventies have rusted with age.

They have gone bitter, that group, because younger women will not listen as they warn of 90-hour weeks for women and almost total responsibility for children. The golf they thought would be the final bonding activity with the men at the top is now becoming the occupation for their retirement years. They talk of balance in their lives, of downsizing to achieve real happiness, of getting out of the rat race because they have real values.

The first famous one who talked like that was profiled everywhere and chat shows resulted. The second one registered on no Richter scale of public awareness. They talk, the ones disappearing from the financial institutions and the big commercial bodies. They talk, the women extruded in mergers and acquisitions. They talk to themselves, because nobody else listens. They take the ambitious minds that dreamed of ruling the world and devote them to reflexology and aromatherapy.

Sometimes, worst of all (worse even than reflexology), they talk of menopause. There's Cybill Shepherd in the US, her television series axed, now discovering the beauties of menopause and talking to any media outlet that will have her. The ones who talk of menopause make the worst choice of all. They ask, rhetorically, why nobody ever talks of this passage in a woman's life.

Answer?

Same reason nobody talked that much about impotence, pre-Viagra. Why the hell should we have a brisk exchange of our age-related physical inadequacies at the dinner table? I assume Cybill is convinced that because she has been a figurehead of glamour and attraction, this glamour and attraction will flow all over her menopause and she will somehow make the whole thing so appealing, every man within his forties will develop a case of menopause-envy. Yeah, right ...

Faced with the prospect of impending invisibility, women, particularly women who have been famous, once, make extraordinary and counter-productive gestures to get themselves centre-stage again. There's the fifty-six-year-old in Britain, posing in a black satin bra in an Age Concern poster which is supposed to draw attention to prejudice against age. Except that this woman, with her big boobs, draws attention instead to the fact that she is the exception. Of course someone with huge breasts will be tolerable, in spite of being old. But not much more than tolerable, and not even that for long. And what does it say about women with tiddly little breasts when they arrive at the same age? It says, unwittingly, that they will become invisible.

Nobody will see them. A twenty-five-year-old woman driving a car, whether it be a beat-up Fiesta or a convertible BMW, is noticed by every other driver, particularly by every other male driver. A fifty-five-year-old woman driving a car is invisible except as an irritant – "You old fool, get off the effing road."

The electronic mirror, mirror on the wall, the television set, nakedly excludes them. The anchor, if male, can be grey-haired and eye-bagged. The anchor, if female, is twenty-five and dewy as to skin. Women broadcasters over fifty look wonderful on radio or in middle management. Just get them the hell off screen; they might depress the rest of us. You are old, Mother William, the young man said, and your boobs are increasingly slack ...

The potent threat of invisibility hits every woman in every profession. Showbusiness is the tip of the iceberg. But a significant tip. Each of the classic responses shows up. There are the stories about how fitness keeps X young, the stories about how Y is finding her golden years full of unexpected added value, each of them dancing as fast as they can while the slope of the floor gets steeper within every month, decanting them into the open drain of invisible anonymity.

Today, for example, I read a profile of actress Charlotte Rampling saying she's thrilled, in her early fifties, to be less beautiful than she was, and that because she has good bones, she has not yet needed a face-lift. A few minutes later, I'm reading broadcaster Lesley Stahl's autobiography, *Reporting Live*, where the author starts speculating as to how soon after she hits forty she'll need one.

The message is clear. Women aged fifty today have an historic chance of living to be ninety. Built into that benign promise is the malign certainty that thirty to forty of those years will be at best as an invisible second-class species. There, but not there. Existing, but not present. Opinionated but not influential. Talkers without listeners. Displacing no air, casting no shadow.

An exaggeration? Of course. All truths exaggerate the experienced routine.

And you know something else? I am deadly tired of having that bit of poetry from Jenny Joseph quoted at me. The line that goes: *When I am an old woman I shall wear purple ...*

You know why I'm deadly tired of it? It suggests that we can all have a bit of fun when we're old because then we can all be outrageous. So bloody what? What the hell is the point of being outrageous if nobody is watching? Reclusive outrageousness is a contradiction in terms, as is invisible outrageousness.

There was a place, once, in the world for the old and wise, as there was for the old and unwise. Now there is no such place. Radio and television programmes try to ensure that their phone-callers are no older than thirty. Ad campaigns are predicated on the assumption that once you pass forty, you don't spend money, ergo, are not worth anything as a marketing target.

America, on the other hand, has copped on that the over-fifties have a whole hell of a lot of disposable income and that they have the habit of spending. So brand-new markets are opening up in fitness, leisure, adult education, travel and resort-living for older people. (Not to mention incontinence pads and other aids to living, cheerily and graphically presented on prime-time TV in Florida, because so many older people retire to that state.)

To be conscious of all the prejudice against old age while on the edge of it means that every innocent comment becomes a threat. You kid yourself that you are over-reacting, and you know in your shrivelling heart that you're not over-reacting one little bit. You wonder if you should growl and attack every instance of ageism, and you get scared that you will end up dismissed the way "women's libbers" were twenty-five years ago. You wonder if you could in some way be the exception, and immediately feel guilty of a form of treachery to your generation. You decide the generation showing the prejudice is not worth a goddamn, and immediately decide that this shows just how old you are, because nobody except an old person condemns the younger generation.

Even compliments develop a fish-slime underbelly. When someone says you're looking really very well, you parse the upward inflection and decide to resent the surprise it represents. *What, you expected me to dribble and wear a scarf over my thinning hair?*

Another example: you know the way people always say, of a woman who is grossly obese, that "she has beautiful eyes"? I have begun to realize that when people say to you that you have wonderful bone structure, they are suggesting that as age strikes, you will be OK. Except that I know I won't. Garbo had the most wonderful bone structure ever given to a human being, and in her sixties, without surgical assistance, she looked like a parody of a ninety-year-old bag lady. Marlene Dietrich, by contrast, looked better for longer, at first because of face-lifts and later because she used to haul loose skin to the back of her head, stick a hat-pin through it and a hairpiece over it.

Of course, I tell myself, while this may be relevant to an ageing film star, it could not matter to a woman who is fulfilled and has an intellectual life. And, my little internal voice answers, loud and clear: "Bugger fulfilment and my arse to intellectual life: becoming a second-class citizen in the eyes of others ain't no fun even if you think in Ancient Greek and belong in Mensa."

At this point, the only woman I can think of who is still beautiful as she ages is Nadine Gordimer. Still beautiful. Still writing like an angel. I give you Nadine Gordimer.

But Nadine Gordimer I ain't. OK, Phyllis Diller I ain't, either. But, where I stand right now, I am beginning to realize, I can grit my implanted teeth and take whatever toxic waste they throw at me, or go the superficial shallow route and accommodate the idea of surgical intervention.

The idea of a face-lift is beginning to move from the box marked "Freak" to the box marked "Pending".

8

Going for the lift

For the first time, I knew someone who'd had a face-lift. Knew her personally, albeit not well. A close friend mentioned, over lunch, that a TV performer we'll call Bobbi had just undergone a face-lift.

"My husband says it's taken all the character out of her face," my pal said.

"From what I hear of her character, that's probably a good thing," I offered.

She then told me that the newly character-free Bobbi was cutting a swathe through the available Dublin toy-boy selection. On the other hand, she added, that was OK, now that the lift had settled in. But Bobbi shouldn't have gone back to work so quickly. She had done herself no service by reappearing on screen just eight weeks after her surgery.

"That's why the word got around she'd had it," my friend said.

"If she'd stayed away longer, people would have forgotten precisely how she had looked before she went?" I hazarded.

"Not at all. Face-lifts settle in. They just don't look right for six months. You have to take yourself out of circulation for that length of time. You really do."

When I tried to get something more concrete on this idea that face-lifts, like shoes, "settle in", I could find only anecdotal evidence. On the Internet, surgeons scoffed, saying they had patients who had gone back to work, undetected, within weeks rather than months.

They also scoffed at the very idea of a hospital stay. When I had words with Dexy on the subject, she made it sound like the ultimate holiday trip.

"We have this associate relationship with a really good hotel two blocks away," she said. "So you're in luxurious surroundings, not medical surroundings, within hours of the surgery."

"You mean you don't even allow face-liftees to stay overnight in the hospital?"

"Of course not. It's a day surgery procedure."

"General anaesthetic? Several hours in theatre?"

I could almost hear her nodding down the phone as if none of these was a contradiction of her claim that face-lifts were just a matter of a quick drop-in visit, no appointment necessary, walk-ins welcome.

"You're a short taxi ride away," she said. "So you leave the hotel in the morning with a scarf around your face and you get checked, get the drains out, get –"

"Drains? *Drains?*"

Hearing someone do public relations on facial drains is one of life's unexpected treats. Post-operatively, she explained, the patient usually had drains on either side of their face. *As they registered at the reception desk of the luxurious associate hotel, I thought.* But they were no problem. No *problem*, she trilled. They had been no problem to her when she had undergone her face-lift eighteen months previously. She made them out to be roughly the equivalent of disposable contact lenses worn an hour too long.

I recapped to ensure I had a handle on it. Directly after this general anaesthetic, the patient, sutured shut (as to incisions) and trailing drains to right and left, ups and leaves the operating theatre to have a ball, unaccompanied by any medical professional, in the nearby five-star hotel. Right?

She clearly did not like the sound of this, rushing to modify the harsh edges. If, for example, the patient was very anxious, she offered, they can of course get an agency nurse to stay with them in the hotel, but really, it wasn't that necessary. For the first week you really didn't want to be talking to anybody very much, but as soon as the major bandages were off and the swelling had gone down, then you could wear sunglasses and scarves and go for long walks, if you wanted to. Nobody would know you'd had a face-lift.

I allowed as how I would think about that. Which I did as I read a neat little hardback called *Welcome to Your Face-lift*, which had pictures of its honest author before, during and after. Some of the shots taken during the immediate aftermath of the surgery would not only put you off having a face-lift, they would also put you off having a meal for at least twenty-four hours.

"You are drawn to a face-lift like a moth to a flame," I muttered to myself as I viewed the horrific black-and-white photographs in the book.

Cliché, the internal censor hissed.

"Yeah, well maybe it's a sign of age, using clichés."

You think a face-lift's gonna fix that?

"You never know. Remember the psychologists who say if you behave as if you're in a happy marriage, your marriage gets happier. That reality sometimes follows appearance."

Therefore, the way to cliché-elimination is through wrinkle-elimination?

"That's not what I mean."

Well, what the hell do you mean?

"I don't know what I mean."

What you need is a brain-lift, not a face-lift.

"You may be right."

What gives with the easy surrender?

"Age is knocking the fight out of me. Hey, what would you think of me going along with Tom when he's doing his three weeks' consultancy in Florida at the beginning of next month? I have a project I could do on the PC, be at end of a phone."

And?

"And have a little face-lift while I'm there."

So you go back to the condo you and Tom have down there after the surgery?

"Yeah."

And he'll nurse you?

"Not really nursing, not according to Dexy."

Drains?

"We won't think about drains."

That's denial.

"No, that's plumbing."

Does the plumber get briefed in advance?

"The plumber? Oh, Tom, you mean? That's an interesting question."

Hmmm?

"Probably I might tell him I was getting a wee bit of corrective work done. Some phrase like that."

So much for honesty within the relationship.

"Tom is the first to say that it's everybody's daily duty to tell the truth and nothing but the truth; but only an unadulterated bore tells the whole truth all the time."

Oh yeah?

"Yeah."

What you really mean is you're ashamed.

"Of what?"

Having a face-lift.

"I haven't decided to have a face-lift."

Liar.

"But if I did have a face-lift, yeah, I'd be ashamed. I shouldn't be, but I would be. It's sort of a dirty word."

And you've never used a dirty word in your husband's presence?

"Oh, shut up, I feel bad enough already."

Not bad enough to do the decent thing.

"Can't talk now. Must call Dr Brueck."

They said yes of course, it could be done that week. Yes, of course Dr Brueck would be happy to do an arm-lift at the same time. Could I come in next week to have blood tests done? Well, no, I couldn't, because I was kind of a few thousand miles away. This bothered them a little, but with some rescheduling, they established that they could do all the relevant tests the evening I arrived, and assuming all was well, could do the surgery two days later. At dawn.

The basic face-lift would cost £5,500, plus £1,000 for the arm-lifts (engagingly, this was £450 less than if I had been having the arm-lifts on their own – a discount for multiple procedures). Plus there were costs for the clinic and the anaesthetic. Just under £8,000 for the whole lot. I was to send half the money right now, and pay for the remainder on the day I arrived. No chance, clearly, of them being left with a bad debt. Nary a scalpel was gonna get laid on me until I had handed over the readies. *All* the readies ...

By way of exchange for the bank draft, they promised to fax me documentation about the procedure and some forms for me to sign. I stood over the office fax until they arrived.

The first page told me that rhytidectomy (face-lift to you) is a procedure designed to diminish signs of ageing in the face and neck, and in order for it to do that, the patient had to meet a number of rules. You were not allowed to have anti-inflammatory, ibuprofin, aspirin or vitamin E for two weeks before the procedure. (Probably no ginkgo either, I thought, since this herb thins the blood and they're obviously worried about the patient bleeding to death.)

The leaflet went on to promise that the patient would be started on medications the day before surgery. These would include antibiotics and a medication for swelling. The patient was to shower and wash her hair before the surgery, but to use neither conditioner, gel nor make-up.

The second page started with a scream in italics. I was not to smoke and if they discovered I was smoking, I was as good as dead. Assuming I was not caught smoking, the procedure would start with an intravenous line through which medication "to help minimize anxiety and discomfort" would be administered.

The leaflet went on to tell me what I already knew: that the incisions would start at the temple area and go down the ear and backward from the ear into the hair of the scalp. "Underlying muscles and connective tissues are repositioned and excess skin is removed," it added.

Then it got down to serious business, outlining the possible complications. Some of these were cast in vague phrases like "Asymmetry may be present". Don't worry about a thing, was the message, but you might come out of this a bit lopsided. Nothing to do with us, of course. Shit happens. Lopsidedness occurs.

Some of the potential complications were cast as aw-shucks possibilities: "Hematomas due to infusion of blood within the tissues may occur. This may delay healing." I looked up "hematoma" in a medical encyclopaedia. What it meant was that you could get a blood-filled swelling the size of an orange on your face if things went wrong. This just might complicate your speedy return to the world of the normal.

As if wanting to get everything off its chest, the leaflet also mentioned the possibility of developing numbness in the face – "usually temporary but may persist" – thinning hair or nerve injury which would make the patient unable to open his/her mouth. Now there's a great possibility. Get yourself a face-lift that puts your mouth out of business. Speak no evil, sing no evil, eat no evil, ever again. I had not expected starvation as a result of plastic surgery, but I figured I would have read about it if it happened frequently.

The last form in the bundle of paperwork was a series of confessions to be elicited from the patient. The patient confessed that he/she had been informed of all the awful possibilities implicit in this surgery and was still willing to go for it. The patient confessed that he/she had discussed this with the surgeon and had all questions answered satisfactorily. The patient confessed that he/she knew the result of the rhytidectomy might not match what the patient had hoped for, agreed to have his/her photographs used for medical, educational and scientific purposes and had been apprised that earrings were forbidden for three weeks after surgery. (This hadn't struck me before. I wear very large, very heavy earrings. I could quite imagine that they might pull a repaired face adrift from its moorings.)

The patient had to guarantee that they would sleep upright for a week, would have someone to take care of them for the twenty-four hours after surgery and would not gain or lose a huge amount of weight directly after surgery.

I put my pen through the bit allowing them to use pictures of me for educational purposes, signed the form and sent it back. I then told Tom a very limited version of the truth. I told him that I was going to kill two birds with one stone. I was going to travel down to Florida with him and have some loose skin on my neck tightened. He shrugged and indicated he would do whatever was required afterwards. Of course, he had no idea – nor did I – what would be required in caring for someone who had just had a face-lift.

Not that a face-lift was the only thing involved. Let us not forget the question of the upper arms. The vexed and long-term question of the upper arms.

Some aspects of one's appearance are OK when you're young, whereas once you cross thirty-five they are not OK at all. Thin lips are not too bad until the mid-thirties. They can make you look quirky and witty, especially if they turn up at the corners. From early middle age, thin lips make you look like every narrow-minded old gossip you've ever seen.

That said, there is no "good" age at all for fat upper arms. At twelve, I knew this. At twelve, I went to a school which had a uniform, and my view of the school was rendered positive simply because the uniform had a blouse with long white shirtsleeves, whereas another school to which I might have gone had a blouse with perky little cap sleeves. Even at twelve years of age, I had upper arms like hams. Perky little cap sleeves atop my hams would have been so awful, I'd have become a teenage suicide statistic. The long sleeves of the shirt blouses in my school uniform, though, were a cool delight.

Throughout my twenties I avoided all dresses, tops and blouses with short sleeves. I bought coiled-spring exercise gizmos you tucked your feet into and then pulled the handle up so the tendons in your forearms and the blood vessels on your forehead distended. For days after you used it you could pinch the sore muscle under your arm, but even after months of use, if you went to a department store and tried on a sleeveless dress, the swelling rotundities hadn't diminished worth a damn.

If I gained weight (as I did with gruesome ease), did the extra pounds go to my bustline? Naah. Straight to my upper arms, so that even in a jacket, what bulges I had would put you in mind of Schwarzenegger.

When you're under thirty, the fat in your upper arms is the same thickness almost everywhere. Bit like a lagging jacket on a boiler: an even two inches thick all around. But in the years after thirty, it's as if your skin, particularly under the arm, gets fed up being made to carry this weight, and it begins to stretch. To sag.

It still transports the same amount of fat, but now the fat has all come around to the underside of your arm and so your skin carries it swingingly, much as you'd carry a length of wet uncooked dough in a polythene bag.

So I have prolapse of the already fatty upper arm. But there are other women, who have been out running marathons, religiously doing their stretching exercises, staying within five pounds of their perfect weight, and you know what? They don't escape either.

To fix wet-dough upper arms, there's nothing I haven't tried. I've gone to clinics where they strap oval pads on your arms and electrify them, so you see your biceps having 600 seizures while you read *Hello!* magazine. I've done Canadian Air Force push-ups. I've written about "using those wasted five-minute segments of your day when, on the way to the loo or the kitchen, you could casually do a quick round of isometric exercises up against the wall without anybody knowing you're solving the sag". The reality, of course, is that if co-workers or family come upon you trying to push a wall into the next room and letting on you just yielded to a random wall-moving impulse, they think the guys in the white coats should be called.

So, when I'm sitting at the first seminar where the plastic surgeon mentions arm-lifts *en passant* and I go "What's an arm-lift?", I'm ready to stab him because, although he explains it, does he have any before-and-after pictures of it? No.

Odd thing. No plastic surgeon ever shows pictures of arm-lifts. You would have thought, would you not, that patients who might be unwilling to have their faces photographed for comparison

purposes would have no problems having their arms photographed for the same purposes? I mean, how distinctive are
one's upper arms? Who's going to see a surgeon's presentation
and go "Wow, those arms definitely belong to Melanie X"? Who
the hell pays enough attention to anybody else's upper arms to be
able to recognize them at first glance in a before-and-after slide?
After all, if you take a picture below the neck of someone, unless
they have tattoos in famous places, they tend towards physical
anonymity.

I did think about liposuction, but decided that fat was not the
issue. If I stood up and held my left arm out straight at shoulder
level, the saggy bit was almost empty. Reading from the top down,
my arm went:

Skin

Thin pad of fat [acceptable – keeps the skin from wrinkling the
way plastic wrap does when it has nothing inside it]

Bone [it's there, you can feel it]

Muscle [just enough to function]

A great long flapping bag of skin like a pelican's beak.

I could smack it to and fro, the hanging pounch, there was that
much looseness in it, even if I tensed the muscle. If I didn't tense
the muscle and went outside, arm raised, on a windy day, I could
have stood like a scarecrow, arms outstretched, the pouch would
have flapped with every passing zephyr and birds would have
been scared to death.

Imagine a flag hanging from a horizontal flagpole. Throw the
end of the flag up over the flagpole, so you have a flag half as long
as you usually would, looped rather than single ply. Throw a quick
shower of rain so the flag gets gravid with damp. As the wind stirs

the flapping bit of the flag, it (patriotic colours excepted) resembles my upper arm in all its fully sensual appeal.

The truly grim aspect of this was that one could – and regularly did – forget about it. First thing every morning, unless you are a nun in one of those orders that ban mirrors or belong to one of those stone-age tribes who believe you will be struck dead if you look at your own reflection, you get to see your own face, so you tend not to forget how bad you look. But upper arms generally don't come into the frame of the early-morning mirror picture, and so one develops sad little illusions. Bubbles, waiting to be burst.

There one is, wearing the one sleeveless blouse one hasn't given to Oxfam for resale, in the belief that when one wears it, one will remember to keep one's arms glued to one's sides, and one suddenly finds oneself in mid-gesture, hanging skin pouch flapping so freely one expects it to slap one in the face. One's sense of self-worth instantly evaporates.

After this happened a number of times, I took up weightlifting. Never mind took it up: for a few months there I could have done unpaid PR work for weightlifting, I knew so much about its good effects.

No matter whether you called it strength training or weight training, lifting these weights gave you better balance, better mental health as you got older, better sleep at night. It built up muscles, and because muscles are more active than fat, they use more calories, so if I got all my muscles going, I could eat up to 300 calories more per day and not gain weight.

I bought dumbbells. Twice as heavy as the ones recommended, inevitably: dammit, I was going to see results sooner rather than later. (I also learned that you can do much the same thing using big Coke bottles, if you're travelling.) I started to think in "reps", and even bought a couple of body-building magazines filled with shiny women with wide shoulders and sculpted, narrow waists. The only thing that put me off, a little, in these weightlifting magazines was that none of the women had busts. It looked to me as if boobs shrank in response to weightlifting, but nobody ever seemed to notice this or make comments in the Letters sections of these publications.

Every day, I lifted weights. Getting ready for weightlifting took a bit of time, because even the most preliminary exploration of this form of exercise convinced me that instant results were not to be expected and that pushing too fast can rupture you. When you are completely unfit, lifting two ten-pound dumbbells can make the veins in your face pop out, your eyes bulge, your jaw clench and your nostrils flare. And that's only in response to first picking up the dumbbells. When you're lifting them for the sixteenth repetition, and your arms are tiring, what the effort does to your face is scary. On the inside and on the outside.

After six months of this, I had tangible muscle in my arms, but damn-all improvement in the general shape. There was no sign of being able to eat 300 extra calories with impunity. I was also fed up of the whole thing. So around about the time I began to hover, moth-like, around the concept of a personal face-lift, I also began to give serious consideration, for the first time, to the possibility of an arm-lift.

I got the clinic to give me a discount price for lumping the arm-lifts in with the facelift. Having told Tom that I was simply having a bit of skin removed from my neck, I wasn't going to burden him with any of this additional information. Arms were a minor issue, I told myself. The morning of the surgery, Tom dropped me off at the day-surgery clinic before he headed off for his consultancy job.

"I'm not under pressure after lunch," he said as I got out of the car. "You can ring me whenever you want to be picked up and I'll get over here in a jiffy."

In the day-surgery place, they prepped me, got an I/V into me, and then added general anaesthesia. I knew no more. I knew no more, even about Tom's return. I had given the nurses his phone number, because they said they might like to call him while I was still drowsy in the recovery room. As it turned out, "drowsy" didn't begin to describe what Tom found when he arrived.

I don't think he will ever get over it.

I'd gone in, remember, mentioning in an offhand way that I was going to have some loose skin removed from my neck. He came into the recovery room to find nobody he recognized there. The nurses indicated one bed and for a moment he got ready to tell them some mistake had been made about identity. That apparition on the bed had nothing to do with his wife.

That apparition had a huge white inflated doorstopper tightly bound around her face, which was swollen to three times its size and coloured a mixture of puce and purple. In addition, the apparition had tubes filled with blood coming out of the left and right sides of the doorstopper bandage, and a square patch of what looked like road rash on its forehead and mouth. It further seemed to be wearing a straitjacket that tied its upper arms to its trunk.

The only thing he recognized was my hand. He sat down beside the bed because it was considerably easier than standing, if he had to look at this horror.

"At the present time, your wife is a little drowsy," they said, smilingly.

He tested this out. I was self-evidently unconscious, rather than drowsy. Not to say poleaxed. Not to suggest comatose.

"Before we walk her to the car," they said and he laughed.

"You can't be serious," he said. "You think you're going to walk her to the car?"

They allowed as how they might take me in a wheelchair to the back door, but that I would then have to walk from the back door to the car. However, moving swiftly along, they said, let us tell you what you have to do in the way of post-operative care. Because you are your wife's carer, you know. Tom said afterwards that this established for him their view that if he was so astonished by a little swelling and colour-saturation, he probably wasn't much of a carer and had maybe failed to read the literature completely. He did not tell them that he had read nothing of the literature because his wife was so busy letting on that there was damn-all happening other than a little skin tweak.

"Take me through it in detail," he said.

He then underwent an hour-long tutorial on how to remove and replace drains, how to clean suture lines, how to recognize symptoms of excessive swelling or high fever. He glanced across at the horror on the bed when they talked about excessive swelling, but the nurses said that what he was seeing was perfectly natural, even satisfactory, and that all he would need to do was keep me elevated and surround the dressing with ice.

They even had a clever device to help him do this last task. It was like a medieval nun's head-dress: white cotton on the outside, plastic on the inside. A bit like two lungs in shape – one lung to go down the left side of my face, the other lung to go down the right side. You opened the snap fasteners at the bottom of the cotton, then opened the plastic, which was held in a sophisticated plastic clothes-peg device, inserted ice, and then positioned it firmly around the padded bandage. Tom indicated that he thought he could do that. They gave him the medieval head-dress, a dozen replacement drain-vials and a few other bits and pieces.

He put them in the car and took the car around to the back of the day-surgery centre, thinking bitterly how patients might be admitted through the front door when they looked normal, but were discharged out the back door when what they had done to you made you look like an unnatural disaster. When he got the car lined up and had opened its back door, he spotted that they were waiting there, with me in a wheelchair, one of them standing behind the wheelchair and holding up my head, which otherwise would have nodded forward.

"How the hell am I going to keep her head up in the car while I drive?" Tom asked.

They glossed over the question, instead making reassuring noises and telling him to take a leg, there. The nurses and Tom got me into the car. They moved the seat-back so that I was tilted backwards, and then tied me gently in place with torn towels. Tom was glad that the condo where we stay in Florida wasn't far away, because if it had been a long journey, he was sure someone would have reported him to the sheriff's office as transporting a murdered body in a moving vehicle. He got a few strange looks even on the short journey.

He was also glad that we have a ground-floor condo, although getting me upright and in through the front door of it took him fifteen minutes. Then he had to arrange pillows and other obstructions to ensure that I could not slide down in the bed.

He had achieved all this, cooked and eaten a meal, worked through his notes for the day and gotten used to the full horror of this moon-shaped swollen monstrosity before I began to come to.

Even when I was semi-conscious, he said afterwards, it was difficult to tell, because my face was so swollen, my eyes could open only a slit, and my mouth ditto. For an innocent bystander like him to spot the difference between eyes slitted in sleep and wakeful eyes slitted only in response to swelling is quite a challenge. It took him a while to note that even slitted eyes, if wakeful, blink, and so if there were twitches below the eyebrows, that meant I was awake. Of course, this drew his attention to my eyebrows, which he said stood out from the swelling as if at the limit of their endurance. He kept expecting them to pop off from pressure.

To fill in the time between when I began to show faint signs of life and when I was sufficiently awake to say the odd monosyllable, he searched the kitchen for anything which might make feeding me a little easier. He found one of those athletic drinking beakers – the kind that marathon runners use, with a big fat drinking straw of concertinaed plastic. He made an oversized cup of tea in the beaker, which is exactly what I needed when I woke, parched.

He sat on the side of the bed, holding the beaker and looking at me. It required an enormous effort to keep my fattened eyelids open, and so for the most part I sat there with my eyes shut, listening to Tom breathing heavily.

He breathes heavily when he disapproves of something. On this occasion, he did such committed heavy breathing over such a length of time that I eventually patted away the drinking straw for a moment and asked him what's wrong. Never mind, he said, and inserted the straw in my mouth again as if I was a baby. Why, I wondered aloud, easily distracted, did the sides of my eyes hurt?

Of course, what I don't realize is that half the time when I'm sitting there thinking that I am wide awake, just have my eyes closed because their lids are fat and hot and heavy, I am drifting off to sleep. Each time I do, Tom takes the straw out of my mouth. Then I hear him breathing again and I ask him what's wrong and he says never mind and puts the straw back into my mouth and because the drinking beaker is sort of double-glazed, thermos-fashion, the tea is still hot, and so I have the illusion of continuity, although probably this goes on for an hour or so.

Eventually, the tea, or what's left of it, becomes lukewarm, and I put the straw away and start to get out of the bed.

"What the hell are you doing?"

I open my eyes and see Tom, or a thin lateral slice of him, looking horrified.

"I need to go to the loo," I say, trying to understand why he seems so rattled by something so normal. I can hear the beaker being put on the side table.

"You are not to go anywhere out of that bed without me minding you," he says fiercely. "Is that clear?"

I nod.

"You are not to nod, either."

Since he has told me not to nod, I sit there not doing anything.

"You are definitely not to nod," he says.

I try shaking my head from side to side, but that hurts, too. He pulls off the bedclothes and guides me into a sitting position on the edge.

"Hold on to me."

I think this is all very sweet and excessive and then starbursts of light explode behind my eyes and a sound like an ambulance having sex with a hoover fills my head.

"See?" Tom's voice says severely.

I wonder how he knows about the sounds in my head and that makes me laugh.

"What's funny?"

"Ambulance and hoover having a bonk in my ears."

"You're bloody delirious as well," he says, furiously.

"Why you cross?"

"Never mind why I'm cross. Turn right; this is the bathroom."

"On my own."

"What?"

"Privacy."

"Privacy my ass," he says and pulls down my pants.

"Contradiction," I say. "Go 'way."

He takes my right hand and locks it onto the sink, then takes my left and I know I'm holding the bath.

"I'm going to leave you for precisely two minutes," he says. "You are to pee and not open your eyes or do anything else. Is that clear? For Chrissake, stop nodding."

I think about standing up by myself, but he is back before I can, and has me sorted out in a second.

"Want to see myself."

"You don't, actually."

"Do so."

"Put your hands flat in front of you."

I obey, and steadied, open my eyes as much as I can. In the mirror, there is a huge thing circled by a padded thing like you see around the neck of someone with whiplash – that thick and inflated. It goes from chin to the top of the head – all around like the tyre on a wheel. Because it is so big and because I am so swollen, there is no hair to be seen behind it, so it acts as a huge frame for what used to be my face. It is purple in some places, bright burned red and weeping between my eyebrows, and inflated so that I have no features – my nose is splayed and sunk in the middle of all this taut, shining purple.

There is bruising so sharp it looks like bleeding in the folds at the sides of my eyes, and my eyelids, particularly the top ones, are so fattened by swelling that maybe an eighth of an inch slit is all I can see of my eyes, but they are as bloodshot as hell.

My mouth is not only swollen, but pressured by the swelling all around it so that I look like an African-American determined to blow a kiss. Except the lips are so swollen they're stuck together. Behind me in the reflection in the mirror is Tom's face, looking small, normal, worried and infuriated. He says something I don't quite hear; this is because of the padded white bandage, which covers my ears. There is a flex going down each side of my neck, disappearing into the front of my shirt. Without thinking, I raise my right hand to touch the flex and the starbursts happen again.

"Drains, is what they are," Tom says, turning me around and getting me moving back towards the bed. The cool smooth feel of the sheets fills me with relief and comfort. I start to slide down in the bed.

"Sit up. You're not allowed to lie down."

He pads me into position with pillows, and I must drift for a moment or two, because the next sensation I have is of milk bottles being removed from my bra. There is something deeply unnatural about this, and I resist.

"Stop it," Tom says. "I'm removing your drains."

By now he knows that I want to see what's going on, but have a limited slice of vision. So he holds up two six-inch vials with rubber stoppers on the top of them. They are filled with my blood.

"I have to milk them. Hold still."

"Milk them?"

"Yeah."

He squeezes the flex leading into each drain, starting up at my ear. The process makes the most extraordinary sucking sound inside my head. Then he removes the two vials and replaces them with new ones. When he has the new ones attached, he stuffs them into my bra.

"Did they tell you to do that?"

"No, they told me to Elastoplast them to your chest."

"Bra's better."

"Bra's definitely better."

"Hungry."

"Well, you're going to have to stay hungry. I have another thing to do. Don't move until I come back."

After one of those little intervals that may or may not be sleep, I hear water sloshing.

"Hungry," I say.

"It'll have to wait. I have to wash your lesions."

"What lesions?"

"The laser lesions."

For some reason, he reverses the hard and soft "s" sounds in this, so what he actually says is "The laysher leezons." This makes me laugh even while he's gently pushing me forward, and then there is this searing sensation as if he has thrown sulphuric acid between my eyebrows.

"Waaaah – Oh, for – Oh, God."

"Hold still."

"Waaah."

"Hold still, it will be over faster. Now, there's the worst of it. Pat it dry yourself."

There is a big soft towel in my hand and I touch it softly off the roasting roaring pain.

"OK, that's enough. This is ointment."

I shrink away instinctively, but the ointment immediately reduces the pain a bit. Plus the heat from the lesions instantly melts it and makes it easy to spread.

"Now, you're done. What would you like to eat?"

Because the pain between my eyebrows is only beginning to reduce in volume to a dull roar, as opposed to the full-voiced scream up to now, I indicate that the hunger has gone off me. He sloshes away with what I assume is the bowl of water he used to wash me with. I touch my cheeks. In fact, I get the feeling that I have only to raise my hands halfway to my face and I will find myself touching my cheeks, they are so swollen.

"Lift up your face. This won't hurt."

The kindness of the warning makes me cry, but the salty tears hurt the skin of my face. Blindly and silently, I lift my face and he loads the two donkey-bags of ice around them, tying them front and back snugly, so that the coolness begins to seep through the bandage to the swollen tissues.

A few minutes later, he is back.

"Open your mouth. Three capsules."

"What for?"

"One for pain, one for swelling, one antibiotic."

I open my mouth and capsules, followed by water, go in. A soft cold face flannel is held over my eyes and the relief is wonderful. I lift up my hands and hold on to his wrist. His hands start to pull away the flannel, thinking that's what I want, but I pat his wrists and we sit there, me hanging on to his wrists in silent gratitude.

"Jesus, Tess," he says when he's turning the flannel over in order to put the cooler side to my eyes. "*Nothing* could be worth this."

"I'm sorry."

"I don't mean for me. I mean for you."

You're right, I think, drifting off on a tide of codeine. At odd times during the night, I wake to find myself being tended. Once, he seems to be walking around the bedroom for a long time, but my eyelids have swollen so much that I can get not even a sliver of vision through them.

"What are you doing?"

"Getting dressed. I'm going out. There's a twenty-four-hour 7-Eleven near here."

My mind ties itself in knots over a twenty-four-hour 7-Eleven. While I believe I am still concentrating on trying to work it out, I can feel his weight on the bed and his voice comes close to me.

"Terry? Wake up."

"Am awake."

"You've been to the loo, you have fresh ointment on your face, there's a drink" – here he takes my hand and guides it to a round cold surface – "within reach. You are not to leave the bed. You don't need to leave the bed. You have no reason to leave the bed. I will be not more than ten minutes. Are you with me?"

I promise I will not leave the bed, and drift off to sleep instead. Which means it seems only a second later when I find him putting something fat under my chin.

"This," he says crisply, "is your travel pillow from the plane."

Yes, I think. The broad U-shaped thing you blow into to inflate.

"I'm putting it on back to front to support your chin. I've been watching you slide down and it's not going to do the shape of your face any good. So don't pull it out when you wake up and become aware of it."

Some mad reference in my head reminds me that the young Queen Victoria had to wear a sprig of holly at her throat to make her keep her chin up because she was small, dumpy and unregal. I wish to convey this reference to Tom, but the connection between my memory and my tongue is temporarily out of service.

"These are frozen peas," Tom says.

The most soothing coolness arranges itself around the sore hot swelling. I indicate this is wonderfully different to anything he put around the swelling before. He indicates this is why he went to 7-Eleven. I tell him he is an awesome husband. The light goes out. I wonder if I have managed to articulate the comment about him being an awesome husband, and for safety's sake, repeat it.

"I heard you the first time," he mutters sleepily. "Doesn't detract from the fact that I am married to a frigging lunatic who currently looks and sounds like a helium balloon."

I think I laugh at this, but am asleep before I am sure.

In the morning, Tom takes me, swathed in scarves, to the clinic for them to remove the big padded bandage. My eyes have gone back to being half-closed rather than totally closed, but the rest of my face is taut, hard and hot to the touch. The surgeon seems inordinately pleased with everything, however. When Tom says that the drains had to be changed much oftener than he had been led to expect, the surgeon makes crooning, Oh well, noises in his throat. This annoys the hell out of Tom.

"Not to put a tooth in it, my wife bled like a stuck pig," he says.

The surgeon points out that this was only from the head wound, not from the arm wounds. Tom, who has forgotten to check the drains from the arm wounds, is silenced by this, and the surgeon uses the opportunity to point out that he did some laser work on me as well and that there is no extra charge for this. That's the marvellous thing about medics who do elective surgery, particularly Americans doing elective plastic surgery. They are so informal in places, like admitting to anaesthetic opportunism: "Hey, we have this broad unconscious, let's laser the hell out of her face; she's signed a form so loose, it allows us to change the colour of her eyes if we chose. And do it for free, too." You cannot imagine a surgeon on the other side of the Atlantic telling you what a bargain he has just given you by throwing in a fast bit of laser for the price of your regular face-lift ...

I think the surgeon adds that the skin where he has lasered it will be red for six months, but I do not reflect on the implications of this. I have enough to cope with right now.

Me bandaged up afresh, we head to the car. I am able to walk without much difficulty, and am feeling positively chirpy. Tom, having spent the night preventing me from choking or bleeding to death, is considerably less than chirpy. He also does not like the idea of leaving me in the condo on my own all day, and says he will come home for lunch. I can, I tell him, offer him a pleasing assortment of thawed frozen peas. He snorts and gets me back into bed, puts radios, phones, painkillers, drinks and frozen peas within my reach and goes to work.

Although I am no longer hung over from the anaesthetic, there seems little to do but sleep, and so, listening to music on the radio, that is what I do for most of the morning. He comes home at lunchtime to refresh both me and my supplies.

"Should you still be that swollen?" he asks reassuringly as he heads out the door to his afternoon session.

The same question had occurred to me. Now that I am able to wander around the apartment safely, since there is no remaining light-headedness, I have examined myself (holding my eyes open with my fingers) in the bathroom mirror, and I am like one of those display apples you see in supermarkets: bright red, hard as a rock, shiny from polish. The swelling comes burgeoning out from under the bandage and I am beginning to think the bandage is cutting off my circulation, but the recurring warning given (verbally and in writing) was that, no matter what happened, the patient was not allowed to cut the bandage.

Eventually, in desperation, I ring the clinic and get talking to a nurse who asks me to quantify the swelling. How the hell do you quantify something that makes you look like a mad red smile badge? I figure my face is twice its normal size. I look like a horror baby out of a Stephen King movie. A baby because every bit of expression, every bit of knowledge, experience, wisdom and cop-on, is removed by the swelling.

I had never thought of swelling as erasing character before, but it erases everything except an increasingly shiny, increasingly taut surface. In fact, I tell the nurse, I am afraid if I stuck a needle anywhere in my face, it would explode. When she tells me earnestly that this will not happen, I have to remind myself about how very literal-minded Americans are.

"I know it won't explode," I say. "But I'm running out of frozen peas and I ca—"

"Pardon?"

"Frozen peas. Bags of. To reduce the swelling."

"You shouldn't be still using ice after eighteen hours. You are constricting the blood vessels and the swelling cannot reduce if the blood vessels are not dilated. You should be using mild warmth, if anything, at this stage."

This is a great relief to me. I spend a lot of time in the bathroom running warm water over sponges and face towels and applying them to the edges of the swelling. Every hour, I have to wash off the ooze from the laser surgery, because if you leave it longer than an hour, it forms a crust, which (according to the new leaflet the surgeon handed me as I left the clinic) all too easily provides a breeding ground for bacteria. The routine is that you wash it off, which is agony, pat it dry, agony times two, apply post-laser ointment, agony minus three.

Eventually, some of the tightness in my face recedes. When Tom comes home in the later afternoon, he looks quite relieved.

"I wouldn't say you look human," he says. "But close to it."

I still can't open my eyes or mouth fully, and my hearing is a little impaired by the bandage, but there is nothing I need Tom to do for me, and so he turns in early. Obviously, the previous thirty-six hours have had an impact on him. A light sleeper at the best of times, he is now so wary that if I as much as sneeze, he is halfway upright asking what's wrong and reflexively telling me not to get out of the bed.

What fascinates me is that, although my face demands an extraordinary amount of attention and assuaging, my upper arms give almost no trouble. There is virtually no swelling and damn little discomfort in them during the days following the surgery. The discomfort – and it is no more than that – is a bit like what happens when you have done too many reps with a couple of ten-pound dumbbells: you are unwilling to raise your arms above your head, because the smallest movement reminds you gently but inexorably of recent trauma.

For a couple more days, I peroxide the stitches to keep them sterile. When the peroxide hits, it fizzes gently. At this stage, I have baths from the armpits down, but cannot wash my hair, which is mucky. When I go back to the clinic, they take out every second stitch in the face and neck, followed the next day by the other stitches. This means I will be able to wash my hair, about which I have a quite disproportionate sense of relief.

They also take the stitches out of my arms. When they do this, I am somewhat taken aback. The bit being held together by the stitches is not where I expected it to be. I had thought it would run down the back of my arms, the way the seam runs down the back of one of those sexy stockings. But no. The cut has been taken on the inside of my upper arm, so if I raise my arm I can see it immediately. I ask why the hell it's done that way. The surgeon looks astonished and says it's always done that way. Which, I point out, doesn't answer my question.

He gives me some answer, to which I don't listen, because I can see that the incision goes only halfway between the armpit and the elbow. Why, I ask, does it not go the whole length of the arm? Ah, he says, obviously deciding he has mollified me about the centrality of the scar, that's because the slack can be taken up using this quite limited incision, as opposed to something more damaging. Again, I'm not listening to him, because I'm examining my own left armpit while he swabs peroxide on my right arm.

The incision starts on my torso just under my armpit, goes through my armpit and then down my arms.

"You can gauge how much tissue was removed, there," the surgeon says, nodding to my left armpit.

It is astonishing. The entire hair-bearing bit of my armpit is gone. He must have taken away four inches of skin in the armpit area and maybe three inches of skin further down my arm. There is no longer any movement – any looseness of flesh flapping freely – under my arm. That's the positive side of the situation. The more negative side is that, once he has taken the stitches out, I have a livid purple scar down each arm. If I were to do an out-thrown arm gesture like "Welcome!" it would astonish, even terrify, those being welcomed, because it would reveal these two scars. The surgeon says they will fade; that in a few months' time, I will hardly notice them. Hmm, I think.

Anyway, there is nothing more the surgeon needs to do for me, right now. I am safe to travel on a plane, although he admits most people do not go back to work ten days after a face-lift. I am planning to go back to work eight days after a face-lift, but I do not tell him this. One of the reasons I want to go back so soon is my conviction that if you have been away for less than two weeks, nobody would ever suspect you of having had cosmetic surgery. The only problem is the laysher leezons, as my husband keeps calling them.

The surgeon says that in a few days I should be able to use concealing make-up on them. Green is the best for damping down the redness. I buy green make-up. I also change the frames in my specs, on the basis that this will confuse people.

Finally, I get an extra-short haircut, because if anybody does get the idea I have had a face-lift, they will be expecting me to wear my hair longer to conceal the scars. Not that I'm paranoid or anything.

In the event, my skin is too damn sore to tolerate much of the green make-up, so I dye all the bits around the laser lesions with instant tan, several coats of, and then use bronzing powder over the whole lot. The result is the appearance of bad sunburn, concentrated in a couple of areas. This leads to lots of comment in the office. I get asked if I fell asleep in the sun. I admit nothing but look sheepish.

"You really should take more care when you go to the tropics," I get told solemnly. "You look like you really overdid the sun. Your face is slightly swollen, even."

By the time the lasered area is tough enough to withstand make-up, the swelling is gone completely, and people who had been (fortunately) distracted by the burns now tell me it must have been a great holiday, because I look better than I have for years. I make sure to act surprised and gratified.

The next phase is people telling me I really have very good skin and I should take care of it, not get sunburned as badly as I did. Before the face-lift, nobody ever told me I had very good skin, because I had that softly crumpled skin age gives you. I concentrate on behaving, in response to their good, if tangential advice, as if I was acknowledging a long-established ownership of high quality skin, all the better to take care of, my dear.

The laser tones down to normal colour, and I have to admit that the resurfacing is very effective. Wrinkles much reduced, skin brighter, younger, even thicker, if that's possible.

The face-lift leaves a series of sensations that fade over time. But "over time" means four or five months. There are tingling attacks when one side of my face becomes electric with what feels like pins and needles. There are numb patches which regain their feeling not gradually, but in sudden bursts, so that it feels as if one coin-sized portion of a cheek is making a major statement.

There are pleasant pains. Difficult to explain that last one, but it's the case. One's face seems alive in a way it never was before. Bit like when you come out of a very cold seawater swim and it feels as if you have nerve endings where you never knew you had nerve endings before. It is enormously pleasurable to feel one's face coming to terms with its new configuration. In fact, to be honest about the whole thing, these sensations are more pleasurable than most other sensations I've experienced through my skin. I wouldn't say I would have another face-lift just to go through them again, but I sure as hell miss them when they quit.

The downside, if there is one, of the face-lift, is twofold. The first is that I develop quite lumpy scars just behind the hairline at the back of my ears. This, I understand, is partly because I am genetically predisposed to keloid or raised scars. Hairdressers ask me if I had an injury. I tell them I had a car crash. (I did, too. Crashed into the gate-post the week I bought my new car and didn't do the front offside any great favours, but no damage to me. However, people will take the most delightful unjustified inferences out of such a statement if you leave them to it.)

The other disadvantage to the face-lift is that, now that the section of my face below my eyes looks fresh and dewy, as if I had binged on vitamin C and had a great night's sleep, it is more noticeable than ever that my forehead looks like a ploughed field (smooth soil shows where the laser hit, but even a CO_2 laser cannot cope with the deep astonishment wrinkles) and that my eyebrows are sunk over my eyes as if I had just been told the end of the world was nigh.

Of course, it could be said, and no doubt *would* be said by the plastic surgeon, that one of the main reasons people do not assume I have had a face-lift is because they look at my forehead and its wrinkles act as instant disproof of any such possibility.

I am doubly glad, as the months go on, that I admitted nothing to anybody about this surgery. A face-lift improves for the first six months, as tissues pull up and tighten. Therefore, you really don't look your best until after those six months. In the fairly direct aftermath of surgery, you look good, but not so perfect everybody would immediately spot what happened. Your appearance improves from day to day, but in such small increments that even though they are there to observe you, they never notice anything. They simply believe you're taking better care of your looks and it is paying off.

General level of satisfaction with face-lift, then, very high. Nine or ten months after the surgery, I enthuse to Tom about it and ask if he cannot see the difference it makes.

"I liked you fine the way you were," he says heavily. "I don't see that much difference. I think it was the most bizarre self-mutilation, and if that makes you happy, OK."

"Are you still hurt I didn't tell you the truth in advance?"

"Hurt? I was never hurt," he says, looking astonished.

This, I guiltily realize, is quite true. He is insufficiently self-regarding to see my secret-keeping as in any way diminishing him. He does not even see it as insulting to him, because he knows (a) I wouldn't insult him, and (b) even if I tried, I couldn't. You can only insult someone who's not sure who they are and what their value is, and my husband is pretty damn certain on both counts.

"On the other hand," he says, "I was pissed off at you and still am for leaving me so unprepared. I could have done you permanent damage if I hadn't listened to those nurses. *You* could have done yourself permanent damage if I hadn't copped on pretty quickly that we were dealing with the results of major trauma."

"I'm really sorry."

"Next time, brief me, OK? I won't tell anybody else. But I can do without having to speculate, any time I travel with you, about whether or not I'll get you back at the end of a day covered in blood and bandages or normal."

I promise him proper briefing the next time. Not, I hasten to add, that there was likely to be a next time.

"Mmm," he says. "What the hell got into you, thinking you could conceal a goddam face-lift and two goddam arm-lifts from me?"

"I concealed them from everybody else."

"Everybody else is not your husband."

I still feel like hell about that. It's the only aspect of the face-lift about which I do feel bad. In general, the thing has been positive to heavenly.

COST: Eight days' incarceration, £8,000		
VERDICT: Face-lift	10 out of 10
Laser re-surfacing	10 out of 10
Arm-lift	5 out of 10

The arm-lifts are a different matter altogether, although I do not make an issue out of this with Tom. I hope, in fact, that because he did not get so physically involved with the arms as with the face, he may have forgotten I had this done at all. But I had it done, I know, and I certainly have the scars to prove it.

Six months later, they have faded, but not much. One year later, I have to face the truth. This arm-lift operation leaves me worse off than when I started. Having wanted to be able to wear strapless dresses and short-sleeved tops, I am now absolutely condemned to long-sleeve blouses and dresses. The nearest I can get to an exposed evening dress is one with that chiffon stuff – and even then, I have to use concealing make-up on my two arms.

The removal of the hair-bearing section of my armpit does seem to have a number of advantages, not least the fact that I no longer have to use a depilatory or wax there. In addition, it seems to have done away with the need for deodorant. That's about the sum total of the positives, however. Not only are the scars unsightly, but my right arm has healed in a bumpy way, and both scars seem to be battling gravity, so they are like drawstrings pulling against the skin, creating little v-shaped wrinkles all the way up my arm. In addition, directly below each scar the area has gone soft and flabby, so that the result is actually misshapen. It may not be as bad as it was, in sag terms, before the surgery, but in several other terms, it is worse.

Am I sorry I did it? Yes.

What am I going to do about it? Probably go back to Dr Brueck and say, "Look at it this way, mate. I am not blaming you, because I should have checked all the possible outcomes before I went for this. But, now that I have experienced it and it isn't great, how about going in again, pulling the scar a bit more down round the back, going the full length with the incision so there isn't this soft bit at the end, and seeing if we could achieve a pair of acceptable arms?"

If I did that, then I might – a year or so down the line – look at the possibility of scar reduction, whatever that is.

9

Attacking both eyes at once

Time passes. Eighteen months after the face-lift, the face that meets me in the mirror in the mornings looks the way I would like it to look. I have seen no "settling in", and other than the sensations inside the skin dying down over time, have virtually forgotten I ever had a face-lift.

Amusingly, though, face-lifts have become a more frequent topic of conversation and media coverage. At parties, I hear people talking about particular circles where "you know, all the women have had the lift". It reminds me of the old days when naïve people used to tell you they could spot a gay person a mile off. They always managed to confide this either *to* a closet gay or in the presence of a closet gay undetected by them. Similarly, several wiseacres have explained to me in recent months how you can always spot a face-lift.

"They always wear their hair down over their ears or a bit of their hair in front of their ears," they say. "To hide the scars."

"Oh, you mean like this?" I say, pulling my hair, always combed behind my ears, forward.

"Absolutely," they agree. "Only way they can cover the scars."

"I'd hate that," I say truthfully. "Can't bear not to have my hair swept right back."

I wait until about six months after the face-lift to go back to the dental surgeon to see about having implants put in my top jaw. The reason for the delay is twofold: fear of bank manager, and fear that motor-mechanic-style dental work might pull my newly hung face adrift from its moorings.

The first fear is dampened a little by the arrival of an unexpected royalty cheque. (All royalty cheques are a surprise to me. I am so grateful when someone reads anything I write, I am secretly convinced I should be paying them, and real money to the contrary is always an agreeable contradiction.)

After six months, the second fear recedes somewhat. My face doesn't seem to have any loose bits or bubbles, as in badly applied wallpaper. This in spite of the fact that long after I could have left off the elastic bandage arrangement the plastic surgery clinic had given me, I am still wearing it in bed at night. Just in case I rub too vigorously against the pillow ...

Once I am fairly sure that my face is comfortably bedded down, I go back to the dental surgeon to look at the upper jaw project. In that top jaw are, in all, six of my own real teeth, three at least in the dodgiest of conditions. The first thing the dentist does, having enthused about the way the lower implants have incorporated themselves seamlessly into my bone structure and into my life, is to remind me that the second jaw would be much more time-consuming, costly and bloody annoying than the first. Top teeth are more difficult to implant than bottom teeth.

This is partly because there are natural holes in the upper jaw like sinuses, which do not happen in the lower jaw. Also, I suspect, because gravity is not on your side when you are dealing with the upper jaw.

However, I decide to go ahead, even though X-rays reveal that there has been considerable erosion of the bone in my face, not least because of the car crash, which did away with several of my teeth, thereby removing their capacity to stimulate bone retention and growth.

"What do you do when bone has eroded that badly?" I asked, looking at the X-rays, which of course mean nothing to me.

"We do a bone graft," he says briskly.

"From where?"

"Your hip."

"My *hip*?"

He looks at me in a puzzled way, and I realize I cannot say what I stupidly thought: surely you could take it off the shoulder or collar bone – somewhere nearer where you're going to put it.

An overnight stay in the clinic is scheduled, at the end of which I have a swelling the size of a grapefruit on my hip and a satisfactory bone graft. The swelling is caused by unexpected internal haemorrhaging and takes a couple of weeks to dissipate, during which time I keep having the urge to take my hankie out of my trousers pocket, only to realize that of course the protruding thing isn't my handkerchief but the post-operative swelling. It is neither painful nor dangerous, so I get over it. After much the same interval, he goes in and puts posts (to receive the eventual teeth) into the newly incorporated bone.

However, things do not go swimmingly, this time around.

Several of the new implanted posts fail. They fall out, in other words. Or start rattling loosely around within the gum and have to be taken out and replaced. This causes me endless annoyance, not least because the temporary horseshoe of false teeth sitting on what pathetic posts have got successfully implanted keeps shifting as a screw comes loose. When this happens on a business trip I have to go to an overseas dental implant specialist, who gets cross with me for losing the screw and then screws the thing back with such weightlifter's vigour that I think he is going to pull loose everything lower than my brain.

This aspect of the implants goes on for two years. I feel I am part of a Norse saga that will last several hundred years before I finally get the permanents upstairs. Downstairs is fine. Downstairs I am so used to having teeth that stand on little platforms it now seems perfectly normal to me.

However, before the completion of the implant saga, I begin to consider taking action on my sight. A pal of mine, a few years ago, had diamond surgery on her eyes. The eyes were numbed and a series of pinwheel cuts made in their surface. This changed the shape of the eyeball, radically improved her eyesight and allowed her to go without specs or contact lenses.

At the time, in common with most of my co-workers, I shuddered away from the possibility of anybody cutting into the surface of my eye while I was awake to see it, although I did envy her the fact that she no longer needed lenses of any kind to help her see where she was going and what she was doing.

Then came the Excimer laser. This breakthrough technology

allowed eye surgeons to reshape the cornea surgically without cutting into the eye. They could numb the eye completely by using anaesthetic eyedrops, then in a matter of moments focus an ultra-violet cold light beam on the surface of the cornea, flattening the cornea. The result was that light entered the eye at a different angle, and focus was better. In more than nine out of ten patients, it was claimed, the improvement was to 20/40 eyesight or even better.

Lest you think this information might have resulted from purely academic, selfless curiosity on my part, let me tell you that since I was eight years of age, I have been wearing spectacles so thick you would expect me to be accompanied by a white stick or an Alsatian. If I took off my glasses, I could not safely get to the bathroom in my own house. I could not read a book held eighteen inches away. I could not make up my own face. Goddamn it, if I was more than a foot away from the mirror, I could not recognize my own face.

No matter what glasses were in style, I had a problem. In the days when huge frames that took up half your face were in fash-ion, the implication for me was that you got more space in which to fit more rings indicative of the thickness of the glass held within those frames. Or, more correctly, half-held by the frames. That's one of the problems of really thick glasses in wide frames: by the time they get out as far as the frame, the glass lenses have got so thick, they stick out on one side (usually the inside) of the frame, so if you catch a sideways glimpse of someone like me, you see frame and then untethered glass. It looks extremely peculiar.

But then comes the fashion for John Lennon National Health type frames made of wire. Wire has no coping skills when it comes to thick glass. Mostly, it pops the lens out, so one minute you're having a conversation with someone and the next minute they are looking at you with naked fear, because one window of your glasses has hopped out without warning. Of course, you can't properly see their expression, because half your vision has disappeared.

When you have thick glasses that are actually made of glass, they will not stay in their proper place on your face, but start to slide and, if you don't catch them at the start of the descent, gain speed, take off, and smash on the floor. So as soon as you can, you move to plastic, which is lighter. If you can afford it, you then move to featherlight, which is three times as expensive and half as thick. What is truly dispiriting is investing all you have in featherlights and boasting about them to people who look blankly at you and clearly wonder why you bothered, because as far as they are concerned, you still have specs as thick and ugly as the bottoms of milk bottles.

Of course you move to contact lenses, but there are limitations here, too, if you are both myopic and astigmatic. The first limitation is that you cannot buy off-the-peg contact lenses. You have to get them made up, so if you lose one, a replacement takes time and more money than you have at any given time. In addition, because they are so thick, they clamp on to your eyes like one of those suction gadgets made out of rubber you use to unclog a drain. They are more noticeable from the outside, less comfortable from the inside and when you take them out, you are so short-sighted that even putting on your glasses doesn't make you feel normal.

Hence, when the Excimer laser came along, I decided I could

muster the £4,500 it would cost to have both eyes done and have them done six months apart. This was recommended in some of the literature about this treatment, which suggested that in some cases, one eye might be over-corrected, in which case the surgeon would need to under-correct the other, and therefore would have to laser them at different times.

It soon turned out that Excimer was good for short-sightedness, but major astigmatism such as mine required something more sophisticated called LASIK. The ditsy blonde in the picture accompanying the LASIK biography I eventually turned up didn't look as if she could be trusted with someone's eyelashes, never mind the organs of sight. Even if the biog did say she was a member of the American Medical Association, the American Academy of Ophthalmology, The Castrovicjo Cornea Society (bet they have wild theme parties), the International Society of Refractive Surgery, and the American Society of Cataract Refractive Surgery.

I flew down to Florida for a consultation with her. One of her underlings did the traditional tests of what I could see, using a card with letters ranging from huge to minuscule on a wall about ten feet away.

"This won't take long," I predicted, sitting into the elaborate chair.

It didn't, either. Once I took my glasses off, I couldn't see anything. Not the huge letters, not nuthin'. At first she thought I was kidding her and insisted on going through the ritual of covering up one eye and then the other, but it was quickly established that no matter which way you sliced it, the eyesight issue here was moot, if not white stick. The underling then did all sorts of other tests to find out what the pressure in each eye was, and – having first put in drops to dilate the pupils – took computer pictures of my eyes at close quarters.

"I will now go and print out these pictures for Dr Popowski," she said. "She will be with you momentarily."

Popowski was with me ten minutes later. I suspected I had been left in the marinade that long in order to read the citations framed and glassed on the wall, one of which hailed her as "one of the most experienced refractive surgeons in our community". This is deadly impressive until one seeks a definition of who the community is. Because if it's the 250,000 old folks living in the retirement cluster around this eye-care centre, this does not fill one with confidence. Nothing against old folks, but it stands to reason, does it not, that there wouldn't be that many experienced refractive surgeons kicking around in such a smallish area, and so it wouldn't kill anybody to make the conditional claim to be "one of the most experienced" of that number.

Anyway, as Tom is always saying, experience is not what happens to you, but what you do with what happens to you. Doesn't help me if this ditsy blonde has done three million refractions if two million nine thousand and ninety-nine of them turned out badly. Notwithstanding this sceptical approach to her qualifications, I was nonetheless impressed to find that she – according to the citations – "was a co-investigator for the Summit Excimer Laser trials of Photo-Refractive Keratectomy (PRK) for high myopia", although I'd have been even happier if she had been a co-investigator on something to do with the LASIK laser.

She floated in, all vague smiles and imprecise warmth. Sat at the desk beside where I was planted in the big black chair, and two of the underlings stood reverently at each shoulder. Over her insubstantial silk shirtdress she wore a crisp white coat. My file was opened, and I could see (now I had put my glasses back on) the multicoloured computer pictures of my eyeballs.

"Ooof," she said softly, and turned over some pages.

"Ooof," she confirmed, a few sheets later.

"What does 'ooof' mean?"

She turned around to fully "engage" with me.

"Well, you are aware that you are legally blind –"

"What?"

Flustered by my astonishment, she brought the charts over where I could see them, pointing out the supportive data, which of course meant damn-all to me.

"You mean I should have black glasses and a white stick?"

"No, it is clear you are functional," she said with that earnest literal-mindedness that makes America great. "But there may be a case for welfare support."

I giggled at the notion of being on a blind pension, and then didn't find it funny at all. Not for me. Not for those who are. Shit, I thought.

"Can you fix me?"

"We can certainly improve the situation quite a bit."

"Define 'quite a bit'."

"I'm sorry?"

"Would I be able to do without glasses?"

"Oh, yes, that would be my expectation. The LASIK is producing very good results."

"But you're not sure?"

Oh, shit, I thought as she got launched. I have let myself in for the lecture to the effect that there are no guarantees in medicine, every case is individual, you must read the following six pages and sign off that you fully understand and agree with them, even though they say that this operation may leave you blind, bothered and bewildered, may make your ears hang at right angles, your nose develop noticeable corrugation at the tip and your knees fester.

"I know all that," I interrupted. "I'm asking you what you would expect."

"Very few of my LASIK patients have had to retain their glasses, and even when they did, it was with greatly reduced prescriptions."

She goes on to do what eye specialists always do: draw deadly simple renditions of the eyeball and talk complicated claptrap at the same time. If the cornea is too round, she tells me, or if it's too flat, or if it's off shape in any way, then the incoming light rays either focus in front of the retina or behind it, resulting in refractive errors. Why, I wondered, do doctors always dutifully tell you what is of interest to them? Not only does she do it personally, but she gives me an an explanatory leaflet and a video I have no bloody intention of watching (Jesus, watch eye surgery? Up close? Waaah!).

All I want to know, I tell her, are the answers to five questions:

Q. Odds of throwing away my glasses afterwards?

A. Pretty good. Maybe eight to one against. (These are my odds, based on all the fairly positive noises she makes.)

Q. How long is the surgery?

A. As short as ten minutes, no longer than a half an hour. (It's the set-up and preparation that really take time, although with my problems, the operation itself will be a challenge.)

Q. How painful?

A. Not painful – numbing eyedrops beforehand. Discomfort afterwards manageable by normal painkillers.

Q. Both eyes at once or separately?

A. Both eyes together. Why would I want them done separately? I advance the argument I have heard applied to the Excimer, about over- and under-correction.

She shrugs in a way that suggests anybody as good at laser as she is doesn't get it wrong the first time around.

Q. What price?

A. £1,250 per eye.

Riven with guilt over not telling Tom about the face-lift in advance of it happening, I lay out all the data on this procedure for him. He even watches the videotape that I will not view, and has an enormously positive response to the entire proposal. This surprises me. I ask him why he's not immediately agin it. He explains that, now he's heading for fifty, he has had to give in and start using reading glasses. (Laser surgery does not do anything for this problem, which is one of age.) He hates having to use them and loses one pair after another, probably because he subconsciously wants to lose them.

"I've always felt sorry for you," he says, unexpectedly. "Sterilizing those contact lenses and trying to get them in the morning after the night before. It must be such a pain. Plus, your glasses are so heavy, they dig holes in your face. I would think three thousand quid was a great investment in that sort of situation. You'll probably save it back, over time, through not having to buy new glasses and replace your lenses. But I wouldn't have the two eyes done at the same time. What if it went wrong? Wouldn't you be better to lose the sight in one eye and still have the other to work with?"

Horrified by this grim prospect, I yell at him that I didn't need the shit scared out of me and that he is supposed to be there to be supportive and not to make me feel worse. Furthermore, I say, even thinking about the nature of the hazard turned me into such an abject coward, there is no way I would ever be able to work my courage to the sticking point twice. If I got it near the sticking point once, I would be winning. I test out my face while I talk, finding, with the tips of my fingers, the spots of continuing numbness since the face-lift.

"You still have numb spots since the face-lift," Tom points out with exquisite timing. "Say if you had the equivalent after the eye surgery?"

"I bet if I had told you in advance about the face-lift, you'd have told me to have one side of my face lifted in case it didn't go so well; that way I'd always have the other side of my face to fall back on."

He points out, with quiet self-restraint, that since I hadn't told him I was having a face-lift, and therefore had not permitted him to share his thoughts in advance of the surgery, it was not fair to extrapolate from the quite different endangerment (his actual word) represented by eye surgery and to attribute, retrospectively, an illogical and irrational view to him.

"Anyway, if I have both eyes done at the same time, will you mind me afterwards?" I ask, glossing over all that bad stuff.

"Not if it's anything like the face-lift. You should have professional nursing if it's that bad, has that much bleeding. I'm convinced you should have had a blood transfusion, you bled so much after that surgery. I'm also convinced you should have spent at least a week in hospital."

"But look at me now, aren't the results great?"

"I suppose," he says, self-restraint back in action. "I suppose I wasn't really thinking about you, I was thinking about me. If the procedures are less complicated and bloody and don't involve general anaesthetic, yes, I will take care of you afterwards."

"You know what the procedures are like from the video."

"Right, now you mention it."

"Well?"

"Well what?"

"Well, what are they like?"

"If you wanted to know that, you'd have looked at the video yourself."

"I know, but how bad is it?"

"*I* wouldn't go through it."

"Yeah, but you wouldn't go through dental implants either, and you'll end up with awful false teeth, eating mush and dying of malnutrition."

Tom, however, has got absorbed by the technical details of what is likely to be done to his wife's two eyes at the same time. (Or at least in quick succession to each other.)

"They put you on Valium," he opens.

"I don't need bloody Valium."

"It's only one tablet. It's taken about an hour beforehand. I presume to calm you down. However, moving swiftly along. You take your Valium, you get driven by me to this clinic place. They put drops in your eyes that numb them completely. They take you into the theatre and they cut off the front of your eye."

Given the choice between screaming and laughing, I laugh.

"You can't be serious."

Silently, he opens the brochure accompanying the video, and before I can look away, I have hoovered up a graphic of the front of an eyeball – the bit covering the coloured section of the eye in question – cut not quite off, but hanging, like a transparent saucer, by a thread of transparency to the rest of the eye. I begin to whimper at the idea of it.

Tom tells me I need the Valium right now. I tell him I may throw up. He points out that if any of us ever saw an animated rendition of what happens in our insides during digestion of a good meal, we would need Valium and throwing up too. I am getting chills across my shoulders every time I think of someone cutting the front of my eye open.

"The procedure," reads Tom, warming so much to the task of informing and terrifying me that I imagine it must be revenge for me springing a face-lift on him under false colours, "the procedure is called Laser In-situ Keratomileusis. Hence LASIK."

"I prefer LASIK."

"That's only because your dental implants are challenged by trying to say Laser In-situ Keratomileusis."

"Shurrup. Get on with it."

"The eye bod first lifts off the thin layer of the cornea – that's the bit you saw in the graphic. Or you can call it lifting the corneal cap."

"Oh, get off that bit, or I really will be sick."

"Then, 'in less than sixty seconds, ultraviolet light from the laser is used to reshape the internal layer of the cornea with an accuracy of up to .25 microns.'"

"That's a relief. I thought it might be one of those loose careless jobbies where they go as far as .27 microns."

Tom looks at me, startled.

"Irony," I explain. "I wouldn't know a micron if it bit me in the arse."

"'After the tissue has been reshaped,'" he read on, "'the corneal cap is replaced in its original position –'"

"Well, that's such a comfort to know. I thought they'd just sling it back to any old position that suited it –"

"Wait a second, we're coming to a good bit. You'll like this."

"I will?"

"You really will. It says that because the cornea has such fantastic – here, let me get the actual words – 'Because of the cornea's extraordinary natural bonding qualities, healing is rapid and does not require stitches'."

"Stitches? In your eyeball? Oh, God, oh God!"

"I've bloody well just told you there are no stitches."

"That's not the point. I never considered the possibility of stitches. Can you imagine little threads coming out of your eye – not your eyelid, your actual eye?"

"No, I can't. And this thing says it starts healing immediately after the procedure, which only takes minutes. Then it goes on to say that the surgery takes place in a relaxed setting with –"

"I don't care if it takes place in a brothel with a poker game in the corner, for Chrissake."

"So are you still going to go for it?"

"Of course I am."

"Don't shout. Whenever you shout, I know you have doubts."

"I have no doubts. I'm doing it."

"It or both?"

"Both. At the same time. Don't say anything negative, Tom. Just don't say anything."

"It says —"

"I told you not to say anything."

"I'm not saying anything about the wisdom or otherwise of having both eyes done at the same time. I was simply going to tell you that the brochure and the video both stress that you must not wear contact lenses for a fortnight coming up to the procedure. At all. Ever. Not once."

"Why?"

"Doesn't say."

"OK."

"How'll you cope? You hate wearing your specs to work."

"I'll live with it for a week or ten days."

"Two full weeks, minimum."

"Oh, Tom, don't be so literal-minded."

"If I'm doing post-operative nursing, I'm going to be as bloody literal-minded as I want."

"OK, two weeks." We were heading for holidays in Florida within a month, so I booked myself in.

A fortnight to the day before the surgery, I put my contact lenses where I cannot, even by accident, wear them. During the fortnight, people sympathize with me for having sore eyes, but ask no questions.

"Couldn't get the lenses in?" they say, wincing in sympathy with my supposed eye inflammation. I nod. It is, after all, the truth, albeit coming from a slightly different angle.

It slightly surprises me to find a drugstore willing to dispense a single Valium without comment, but they do. Tom supervises me as I ingest it, and then gets ready to make the half-hour journey to the surgical centre where the LASIK laser is kept. By the time we're nearly there, I'm feeling no pain. Not only am I feeling no pain, but although I am certainly still apprehensive, I am suffused with a heartwarming sensation of distance from all trouble. There is trouble in the world. I know that. There are people fighting and dying, I know that. There are boils and warts and burns. I know that. I am about to have the front bit cut off both my eyes. I know that.

But am I emotionally involved in any of these things? Yes, but at a pink-rimmed, sugar-coated, angora-cosy distance. I am so cheerfully verbose, Tom says he must find a way of getting a regular supply of this Valium, although he also wonders aloud, now that we have arrived, if I will be able to walk in a straight line or should he go in and get me a wheelchair.

"Less of it," I say severely.

He grasps my arm in supportive silence to bring me into the lobby, where I am separated from him and brought into the surgical area. Long corridor-like room, with padded chairs lining one wall. I am sat down in one of them. Facing me is a corridor leading off to God knows where. On the left of the corridor is a room with blinds on the glass windows that open out onto the room I'm in. This is where the laser lives. On the right side of the corridor are four post-operative beds. When a nurse comes to put drops in my eyes, I remark on the beds.

"Oh, yeah," she says casually, "very rarely used. Most procedures, people just walk straight out of here. With assistance, of course, because they wear goggles. Now, you just make yourself comfortable while those drops go to work."

I sit, the Valium now having peaked, reflecting on the fact that it is always people who have put you in positions which assure your absolute discomfort who then invite you to make yourself comfortable. You're in the economy seats in a plane, breathing the recycled germs of 300 passengers, unable to smoke, convinced that the pilot is going to head straight for the nearest mountain and drive into it, you are threatened with airline food and magazines in their own plastic straitjackets, and the guy in charge comes on the intercom, tells you a bunch of completely incomprehensible stuff about ground speed and tailwinds, and then says "Sit back, make yourselves comfortable and –". That's another thing. Why do they always tell you to sit back? Who says sitting back is the way to get comfortable?

It is particularly difficult to make myself comfortable in this chair, situated as it is about twenty feet in front of the laser area, from where one can hear technicians, Dr Popowski and their patient talking, and the sound of the machine clanking away to itself. What is most bothersome about the talk is the sense that whatever the hell procedure is underway is not going half as well as one would want. The next most bothersome factor is that the patient is hearing all their ponderings out loud about the problem, whatever it is.

"More drops," the happy nurse tells me, causing me to leap like a stabbing victim, because she has crept up on me without my noticing. I obediently put my head back and she aims at my right eye.

"You missed," I say as she goes on to the left and misses there, too.

I sit up, feeling worried, and she is smiling at me.

"I didn't miss," she says reassuringly. "The first set of drops have worked, is all. So you can't feel the second set going in.

That's really neat – you're well on the way."

When I get back to monitoring the room where the laser has been at work, a victim is being led out of it. She has plastic goggles – flattish and with quite large airholes in them – Elastoplasted to her face and is being led. She is not making any of the agonized noises I expected her to make. She is followed in to the main corridor by a plethora of figures in green. Each has a white mob cap and matching cotton bootees on. One of them is male, weighs roughly 300 lbs and, when he removes the mask from in front of his mouth and nose, has a black beard and moustache. But, with their masks on over their normal clothing, they have a padded anonymity which makes the whole team look, collectively, like the cast of a television series for kids.

One of the Greenies bounces over on soft-shuffle shoes to where I'm sitting.

"So how you doing?" says Dr Popowski's voice.

I try to fit Dr Popowski into these greens and the mob cap. Her Bambi eyes twinkling at me with what seems forced optimism make it easier to recognize her.

"We gonna go do some LASIK?" the 300-lb Greenie asks, putting his mask back on.

"Why not?" asks another Greenie, clapping her little hands.

"Let's do it," says Dr Popowski and I wonder if Tom is within screaming distance and what he would say if I yelled for rescue.

I am taken into a dark room and put on a half-chair, half-sofa. My chin is placed on a platform which is part of the machine. Nurses begin to wind things a bit like those metal wands which screw into place in a Christmas-tree holder to lock the tree into place. Over the noises of my own imprisonment, I hear them debating whether they should start with the left or the right eye.

By now the Valium has worn off completely and I am in tranquillizer deficit, wishing I had taken hyperventilation lessons before I committed myself to this. Hyperventilating improperly is not a good thing. I know, because I am getting dizzy from lack of oxygen and the panic that rises within me is probably not unlike that of an Indian widow catching sight, for the first time, of the pyre on which she is to be roasted in memory of her late beloved husband.

"This will just keep your eye open," Dr Popowski's voice says.

Whattya mean, just? I think.

"For how long?" I ask, and they laugh.

I am sitting here, clamped in this electronic stocks about to have the front of my eye sawn off and they think I'm joking? Oh, Tom, come and rescue me. I'll never have a face-lift again as long as I live. I'll never improve myself in any physical way. I will decay so rapidly, you'll be able to notice and enjoy the deterioration on a day-to-day basis.

The thing that will "just" keep my eye open turns out to be a handcuff. Or eyecuff. It has a round metal section that clamps around the eye. This is not comfortable, but they then complicate things by tightening it. Again. And again. And again. My handcuffed eye is popping practically out of its socket when some unidentified female Greenie pats me gently on the shoulder and tells me I can call out at any time if I feel some discomfort and they will pause. Or even stop the whole procedure. I now have a serious focus for my boiling hatred. You silly Greenie cow, I think, the only way I will get through this thing is if I have no back door. Now, you're suddenly giving me several back doors.

The next voice I hear is a whiskey-and-cigarettes voice, female.

"OK, Dr Popowski's gonna start the cap removal," this voice tells me harshly, at the same time grasping my hand.

"Hold on," the voice orders, and I do.

"Look at the dot," the voice orders, and I do.

Other voices say the laser is going to work.

"Hold on," the harsh voice orders.

I continue to do so, clutching the proffered hand so tightly I'm sure I am cutting off her circulation. Which is definitely what the handcuff is doing to the eye area.

"You doin' OK," the harsh voice tells me, as if it was an order.

"Am I?"

"We're gonna have to go for thirty seconds," says a scared male voice.

"Why that long?"

There is a complicated discussion, into which the harsh voice cuts.

"We got a patient here, guys."

Popowski gets decisive and starts a countdown, tells me I will hear a ticking noise but feel nothing, and orders someone to do something.

"You're doin' great," Harsh Voice says.

Tick tick tick. I keep looking at the dot. At this stage, I would do anything to get the handcuff off my eye. The ticking stops, there is a flurry of activity and before I have fully appreciated the absence of the handcuff from one eye, they are clamping it on to the other. Unless, the Dopey Green says suggestively, I have any worries. My mouth is so dry from terror, I cannot answer this, and so miss my chance to abort the surgery on the second eye.

"Let's keep it moving here," Dr Popowski's voice orders.

Same procedure, same hand, same desperation. At the end of it, they sit me up straight and I sniff the air.

"Something's burning," I say.

"Wuz," says the harsh voice, which, I now discover, belongs to a vast black nurse in her sixties. "You wuz burning. Tha's what the laser does, honey."

I can see light but nothing else. I can feel nothing but discomfort in the skin around my eyes. They sticky-tape transparent goggles to my face to be worn constantly for twenty-four hours, then put bandages over the goggles to exclude light. I am to go home and I am not to look at anything.

If possible, I am to sleep all the time until I turn up at the clinic tomorrow morning for my post-operative check. These (someone folds my hand over a miniature envelope) are strong painkillers, and the amount they're providing me with will definitely see me through the night – there are three or four to spare. The blurriness in my vision will stay for several days.

I ask about the cap. It will have stuck itself back on within a matter of hours, they say. Dr Popowski's voice tells me that no part of the human body heals as quickly or efficiently as the eye. Not many people know that, I say in a Michael Caine voice and one or two of them laugh.

"You were longer than they said you'd be," Tom's voice says.

Several of them explain that I had a really severe vision problem and that this was the reason they had to take such time over it.

"I'm not complaining," he says simply. "I can take her away now?"

They tell him all they have told me, and he takes my arm, warns me of upcoming stairs, and gets me into the car.

"How was it?"

"Awful."

"Awful painful?"

"No, just discomfort and the feeling that they were not desperately sure what they were doing. I'm sure they did know what they were at, but they should be very careful the way they talk in front of patients. Or behind them. Or wherever. If you can't see, you hear doubly well, and it all sounded so ominous. Anyway, it's over. They didn't make any worried noises to you, did they?"

"They said it was a complete success."

"Did they? Oh, good. Not that they'd know."

"Do your eyes hurt?"

"No. But they wouldn't, yet. They're still numb. Carbery's automated movers – we take you from A to B."

"What?"

"That's what it says on a brown lorry over there."

"My God. *I* can't read that easily. How can you see through the Elastoplast?"

"There's a little hole, here, see?"

"And you can read the brown lorry with one eye?"

"All remaining Ford pick-ups at invoice price – the area's biggest selection."

There is a silence while he locates the poster from which I have garnered these words.

"Wow!"

"You can say that again. I don't mind if they scared me. This is fantastic."

"Should you be reading at all though? I thought you were supposed to rest your eyes? Anyway, we're just home and we'll get you into bed straight away. I have a CD player with some of your favourites on it right beside the bed and the radio tuned to a news station."

And that's how it was. Within an hour of lying down to listen to music, eyes closed, I was asleep. About six hours later, I became conscious of soreness, and got out of bed to take painkillers. I snuck a look at both eyes. The right was good, the left less so, in vision terms. In trauma terms, the left was more interesting. Right around the iris of the eye was a blood-line, circular, where the cap had been cut. I covered them up again and went back to bed.

The following day, Tom drove me to the clinic. Sitting in the waiting room, eyes still, obediently, closed, I could hear other patients talking to each other. Several were complaining bitterly about a sensation of broken glass in their eyes. They had been awake all night, they said. Painkillers were useless to combat the misery, they averred. Their eyes were streaming so badly, it looked as if they were crying. Some of them said they *would* cry if they weren't afraid salt water would make the discomfort even worse.

When we were shown in to Dr Popowski's office, Tom mentioned the moaning populace in the reception area.

"Oh, those are the Excimer patients," she laughed. "The Excimer gives rise to between twenty-four and forty-eight hours of real discomfort. In that sense, the LASIK is much easier on patients. You haven't had much discomfort, have you?" This was directed at me, and I had to admit that no, I had not had much discomfort.

The tests showed radical improvement in both eyes, but it would take as long as two months before the improvement settled into place and more scientific measurement could be done. My eyesight might continue to be blurry for several weeks. It all depended. I should come back for a further test – they would sort out dates. In the meantime, for several weeks, I should wear the goggles at night, just to protect my eyes against the possibility of rubbing them when half asleep. I should also ensure that I did not get water into my eyes when washing my hair. The blood circle would fade very quickly. Oh, and I must not play any contact sports or anything like tennis where there was the smallest chance of a ball in the eye. I could now read, watch television, do anything I pleased, with the single proviso that I wear very good sunglasses and a sunshade if I was in bright sunshine.

The only immediate problem I found with this regimen was hair-washing. If you're used to stepping under a shower at full blast, washing your hair and self and getting the entire thing done in a matter of minutes, it is maddeningly time-consuming to have to protect one's eyes from the water.

In the beginning, I tried showering backwards, the way the models are always posed: the water flowing back over their heads so their hair falls down over their neck and shoulders like a mermaid's, even though normally I do it the other way: my hair flowing forward over my face like a troll's. That didn't work well. I tried using diver's goggles – they leaked.

Eventually, I taught myself to shower one-handed, clutching a hunk of face towel to my eyes to prevent anything getting to them. It took more time than usual, but once a new approach becomes a habit, it's as easy as the old approach.

Two months later, I went back. Dr Popowski's response to the tests was a cluck of annoyance.

"We should've put you on the pizza and beer diet," she muttered.

"Pizza and beer?"

"Yeah. You heal too well. We need to have a go at your right eye again. Ella will put drops in."

"Hey, wait a minute."

"No, I don't mean with the laser. I'll just make a couple of incisions, you won't notice it. It won't take but a few minutes."

She was gone, and Ella was anaesthetizing my right eye before I knew what was happening. Ella's main concern seemed to be to reassure me that I would not have to pay extra for whatever Ditsy was about to do to me. If I had thought about it, that might have been a priority, but my main thought was that here I was, getting diamond cuts in my eye, fear of which was just about the one reason I had gone for the laser in the first place.

I was brought into another room, where I was placed, chin on frame. I waited for them to handcuff my eye, but no – the eye surgeon said I would be able to hold it open for long enough. Because my eye was numbed, I could not tell when she had actually connected, and so held my eye open much longer than actually needed. Back to goggles for twenty-four hours, different kinds of drops, one goggle at night for another few weeks, and then – hey presto, I had 20/20 vision in that eye, 20/40 in the other.

The left eye had been left slightly less efficient than the right because, she said, I was coming up to the age where I would develop the need for reading glasses, and she didn't want to speed that by making the left eye perfect, because at the moment, it was

OK on long range, but quite good on short range.

Furthermore, she promised, the human brain was just such a nifty little machine, it would always select the vision from the more dominant eye, which of course would be the 20/20 vision eye. However, here was a prescription and one free contact lens if at any stage I was going to the theatre, for example, and needed to see every expression.

Although I have felt the need to conceal most of the other things I have had done to me, I have no compunction about talking about the eyes. The improvement of one's eyes is regarded as acceptable, valid, worthy, even public-spirited. I even got to feel virtuous, because my local optician's shop had a notice in the window saying that anybody who had old spectacles they no longer used should drop them in to them, because they would send them to the Third World. I had eleven sets of specs in different-coloured frames. Somewhere in the developing world are some awfully short-sighted people looking bizarrely accessorized, but seeing pretty well through the milk-bottle lenses of what were once my glasses. I kept one pair, as a reminder.

Whenever I developed the notion that my eyesight really hadn't been that bad, I would put on the corrective glasses and wince at the way they bent my now almost perfect vision.

I have become quite a proselytizer for this LASIK laser. One of the girls in the office listened to me and followed my path across the Atlantic to Dr Popowski. She turned out to have even worse eyesight than I had once owned, had the surgery, experienced the same terror as they discussed, over her head, the complications they were running into, but found that both her eyes, after the surgery, were 20/20. Not only that, but the shape of her eyes changed marginally, protruding less. When the extra protrusion caused by her old, thick contact lenses was removed, the effect on her appearance was subtly one of improvement. She looked prettier. A welcome, if unsought, spin-off.

A peculiar, if also unsought and somewhat less welcome spin-off for her was insomnia. In the past, the moment she took out her contact lenses or removed her specs, she was in a featureless fog. Now, especially during the long summer evenings – she had the surgery just at the end of the spring – she found herself in a bedroom full of interesting details, overflowing with temptations for eye-opening. The insomnia wore off after a few weeks, and her verdict was even more positive than mine, since no subsequent corrective action at all was required in her case. Best thing she ever did for herself was her verdict.

My own experience was marvellously positive, too.

COST: £2,500 and two days' sleep
VERDICT: 10 out of 10

Great value for the money. Great improvement to my appearance, for several reasons. I no longer have glasses boring holes into the sides of my nose, hurting my ears and making me look like a dragonfly behind a mullioned window. I no longer have badly finished make-up: I can see what I'm at.

No side-effects, no reservations, no bad results. I use artificial tears whenever I remember them, but the very best consequence of the surgery is a mental hiccup I can't get rid of. Late in the evening of a busy day, I find myself resolving to take my contact lenses out soon, because another hour and my eyes will be very sore.

Then I realize I have no contact lenses in – and the perfect eyesight I am enjoying without them will not come at the cost of aching eyes at the end of the day.

Putting on make-up is a joy, whereas before it was a matter of putting on and off glasses, because when I had contact lenses in, it was difficult to see up close. It was also more difficult to put on eyeliner or mascara. Of course, in my pre-face-lift days, I was quite glad to have huge glasses with impenetrably thick lenses covering up the crows' feet around my eyes. But now that the skin there is smooth, thanks partly to the face-lift and partly to the laser resurfacing, there is no need for concealment, and so a peripheral reason for glasses has been swept away. On the other hand, I can now wear the coolest sunglasses, whereas up to now, my options were severely limited.

In addition to seeing much better, I have found an unexpected lessening of sensitivity to light. What I mean is this. When I was hellishly short-sighted and wore contact lenses, perhaps because of the thickness of those lenses, the harsh light in a television studio, for example, or outside on a bright sunny day, was intolerably painful. My eyes simply closed, whether I liked it or not. However, now I can operate in a television studio or outside on a summer day without the smallest problem. Nobody had led me to expect this. I keep thinking I should let the eye-surgeon know about this benefit, but thus far have failed to find the time to do it.

One of the reasons is that the world is so much more interesting and distracting when you can see it clearly. I see small birds, individual leaves on trees, textures and details I have not seen naturally and without some kind of distortion since I was a small kid.

An affordable miracle, that's what LASIK was for me.

10

If I had a hammer(toe)

Tom listened to me telling people about the eyesight improvement for a few months, and supported my telling of the story. Then, one day, he pulled a curve on me.

"You know what I think?" he said. "I think that now you can see everybody's back teeth unaided, you will find new subtleties wrong with your own appearance that you never noticed before and will want them fixed. I suspect this eye surgery is the open sesame to a new set of plastic surgery mutilations."

I ignored him. He was not giving me credit for the fact that I had already rejected – or at least postponed – having permanent make-up applied. The Brueck people had a permanent make-up artist attached to them, and I had sat down with her, having read that Tanya Tucker now had eyeliner and lipstick in place, so no matter how tired or hungover she was, she was made up from the moment she got out of bed. In essence, permanent make-up is tattooing. You can have an outline tattooed on your lips, or you can have the whole lip area tattooed.

The artist admitted that when people have the whole lips done, they have to stay away from work for at least a week, the swelling and weeping is so noticeable and discomforting. Eyeliner is tattooed along the edges of the lashes, and eyebrows are tattooed onto the skin in and around the eyebrows. So if you have short scutty eyebrows, you will not ever have to extend them with eyebrow pencil again.

A number of considerations prevent me falling on this option with glad cries, the first being a certain similarity of shape in the photographs she shows me of outstandingly successful client results. They all have the same mouth: slightly flattened McDonald's arches, rather than Cupid's bow. When I ask her to draw in pencil on my own mouth what the outline job would look like, I end up with these big rounded mountains on my upper lip, as opposed to the more peaky, sugar-loaf shape of my actual mouth. When I point this out, she says that she always does exactly what her customers want (thereby implying that the rest of her customers, clever sane people that they are, choose these hamburger arches and that only freaks like me don't want them) but does not rub out her work and start again to show me she can do what this customer wants.

The very permanence of the procedure frightens me. I have read enough about people like Cher paying a fortune, as they get older, to have the embarrassing tattoos of their youth removed from various parts of their anatomy, to know that removal is neither cheap, easy nor particularly effective. So what if this tattooist makes a mistake?

During the time I am mulling this one over, I become hypersensitive to tattoos of all kinds, and observe that while new tattoos often feature bright primary colours, old tattoos all seem to fade back to a dispirited blue, reminiscent of old carbon paper. While one might live in relative contentment with blue eyeliner, blue outlines to one's lips might be a little offputting to innocent bystanders, and blue eyebrows would put the most unobservant and tolerant bystander off his or her stroke.

I decide to put this option on a back burner for a while, which does not bother the permanent make-up artist one jot: she is booked for the next six months and couldn't have fitted me in, anyway. Is it any wonder the woman can't be bothered to do a hard sell on her upper-lip configurations? And is it not an interesting reflection of the time available to women that they want to shave the couple of minutes off the morning *toilette* even if it requires them to submit themselves to the kind of process drunken sailors have gone for in great numbers down through the centuries?

Instead of having a permanent improvement done to my face, I could, of course, have opted for a moratorium on self-improvement of all kinds. Rather than show such a lack of initiative, I went to the other end of me – to my feet – on the basis that improvements down there might lead, indirectly, to improvements on my face.

What directed me there was the number of people who have asked me if I have a headache when in fact I have not a trace of an ache of any kind. This question has been increasing in frequency in recent years. It is not the done thing to answer, "No, I don't have a headache, but my feet are killing me."

If you admit to sore feet, in my experience, the first thing people do is look at your shoes and ask you what do you expect, the implication being that high heels and elegance are bought at the price of pain and that everybody should go to work in running shoes.

Now, that is one thing I will never, ever do. I buy my shoes by mail-order from a place called Sexy Shoes. The first time I telephoned this corporation, they took my order and then asked if I wanted the delivery made in a plain wrapper to the condo in Florida. I could not figure what could be discommoding or invasive of privacy in the delivery of shoes and said no, they shouldn't bother with the plain brown wrapper. Which of course meant that the mailman knocked on my door and, reading off the package, bellowed, for the delectation of the entire neighbourhood: "Hey, I got some SEXY shoes here for ya."

The shoes from this emporium are tarty in the extreme. They also come in a range of sizes so wide I found it puzzling until Tom suggested they might have a considerable market among transvestites and cross-dressers.

High-heeled pumps, if you buy them in a shoestore, tend to have perhaps two-and-a-half-inch heels. High-heeled pumps, if you buy them from the Sexy Shoes catalogue, have anything from a three-inch to a five-inch heel. As a result, they are a major challenge to stand upright in, and walking is out of the question.

If you ask me why I would want to stock my wardrobe with difficult shoes that inflict enormous pain and make me look as if I'm on the game from the knees down, the honest answer is that they make feet look less like feet. Feet are so awful that anything that distracts from their natural state is a good thing.

Now, I am aware that not everybody agrees with me about naked feet. There are foot fetishists, to be sure. But then there are guys who hang themselves from the nearest rafter and sometimes can't get themselves unhung before death homes in on the orgasm, so what can I tell you?

Not only are there foot fetishists, but a growing number of film and rock stars appear to be convinced that the only way to appear accessible and truly natural is to be photographed in bare feet. I do not go along with this, because I find, when I've read an article headed by such a picture, I have been half-consciously seeking in the text for the reference that will back-justify the naked feet, and a day later, the star's face has disappeared, leaving only an impression of jeans and FEET. It's not my problem, of course. But if there are other readers/consumers out there like me, and I cannot believe I am a raging exception, when in all other respects I am at one with, or a little ahead of, the big trends or preferences of people my age and sex, then I would put it to these stars: is your marketing objective served by being remembered as jeans and FEET?

Despite my belief that feet were a mistake on the part of whoever designed us, and that if He had not been busy making lakes and oceans and food chains he would have realized the right thing to put at the end of legs was a cross between very high heels and rollerblades for women, and straight rollerblades for men, I have become preoccupied, in recent years, by my feet. Skip this bit of the book if it gets you down as much as it would get me down if I were a stranger to my feet.

Here's what is wrong with my feet.

Or perhaps I should start with what is right with them?

OK, here's what's right with my feet. They are small. Women between 5'6" and 5'10" often (results of an informal poll conducted by me when the fancy takes me) have feet of size six or bigger. Me, I have feet of size five or five and a half. That's a Good Thing.

The second positive thing about my feet is a sort of referred benefit: they come at the end of good legs. Even when I put on weight, my legs stay reasonably shapely (let us not discuss the thunder thighs of adolescence) and I have slender ankles which do not swell, as some slender ankles are wont to do, in response to overuse or air travel.

That's the sum total of the good things.

Now, the bad things.

Starting with a high instep. The instep is the big ridge on the top of your foot where a strap goes across if you are a child, or is covered up by laces if you are a running-shoe wearer. With me? Good. Now, some people have a high instep. Either because of overendowment with bone, or because the curve of their foot is very pronounced, the mountain on the top of their foot is Mount Everest as opposed to the moderate hill owned by the average human. I have Mount Everest on steroids. I have an instep so high, assistants in shoe shops call each other over to witness this natural phenomenon.

Straps across the instep I can forget. There is nothing to be done about this. One cannot have one's instep exercised down to normal proportions or liposuctioned away. The thing is an arch of complex bone and that's is. One's instep is a given, in the scheme of things. Learn to live with your instep because it ain't gonna change.

Moving downwards, we encounter toes. Now, here's where the real trouble begins. To take one toe: the stars who have their feet exposed in photographs have toes which are smooth, straight, unjointed. Me, I have toes which have big round lumps at each joint. Each toe starts off promisingly, then suddenly develops this hard round bit, then goes back to being promising, then has another swelling, and before you know it, there's the nail and that's the end of the toe story.

Except there's a codicil. A toe-icil. Each of my toes ends on a platform like an elephant's foot. This is because my toes do not lie down. I have permanently wakeful toes. Other people's toes grow like little flowers out of their footbed and lie fairly flat on the floor until they finish. My toes grow up from the base, start growing across at the first joint, then turn down at the second joint, to rejoin the floor at the end.

Each toe (except the big one, which is too heavy for this lark, and the little one which tries it but goes sideways) is like a fully articulated bridge, allowing air to pass unimpeded under the line of toes. When each toe finishes being a bridge, it needs a platform to get firm on the ground again, hence the funny end to my toes.

This architectural style poses a number of limitations. There is damn-all point, for example, in buying open-toed shoes if the toes on which the shoe opens look like they were made out of Lego by a troubled two-year-old of minimal aesthetic instinct. Consequently, those sexy strappy open shoes with high heels are not to be found in my wardrobe. (I lie. They actually are to be found in my wardrobe, mute testament to the triumph of hope over experience. Every few years I clear them out and give them to one of those places that sell clothes for charity. New, unworn and slightly dated, off they go to find a home with someone who loves them and who has flat toes fit, if not for human consumption, at least for human observation.)

Even in closed-toe shoes, though, my toes have been posing increasing problems recently. The hard bony protrusions are so protrusive, so hard and so very bony that glove-leather shoes take their imprint, and so, even after about six weeks, my expensive high heels stand in the wardrobe with oversize pimples on their top where the leather has gone out of shape to welcome particular bony bits. Don't tell me to use shoe trees. Shoe trees are a snare and a delusion. Shoe trees are a myth like brushing your hair a hundred times at night: there is no objective data to support the claims, but the claims go on from generation to generation. From father to son, mainly. Shoe trees are a particularly bad habit of gullible men. Women have enough to do at night without putting their shoes to bed with springy shoe trees in them.

Now comes the really bad bit. Corns. One does not admit to such things in polite company. One does not admit to such things even in one's own company, let alone go to a chiropodist to get them taken care of. Chiropodists are for one's aged relatives who have awful afflictions like bunions. When one gets a corn, one has a choice. One can buy preparations in the chemist which have tiny oval bandages raised at the sides to take the pressure off the thing. However, this is chiropodist country. Older female relatives who take their feet out of their shoes (there ought to be a law against this, mark you, but that's another day's work) have little oval plasters all over their toes underneath their elastic stockings. Not for a moment, not even if it were to save one pain, could one bear to be seen as part of that societal segment. (So I am an elitist, ageist cow. Think of me as already punished. By foot pain.)

The other option is razor and file. Razor to cut the hard bit off, file to smooth it down. (These files come with a little publicity leaflet saying that filing their feet each day is a cherished essential of the beauty regimen of Swedish women. So?) Just about the only good result from my car crash was that my two feet were not allowed by broken legs to do any work for a year. They came out of the plaster like little newborns. Gorgeous, they were. For about a fortnight. Then they went back to normal.

I cope. But it seems to me that after forty, the skin on one's toes gets thinner or more sensitive. Forty-year-old feet seem to object more to snug-fitting shoes than thirty-year-old feet. Indubitably, they develop hard skin at a faster rate, this hard skin, paradoxically, producing spearing pain underneath.

When I find myself, in the early morning, factoring these realities into my choice of what I will wear for the day, I know I'm in trouble. I want to wear the peony suit with the matching four-inch heel pumps, but my face scrunches up at the thought of the inevitable pain. It will, that pain, be bad by lunchtime, excruciating by dinner time, so bad by going-home time I will kick off the shoes, drive barefoot and even engage in an argument with myself outside my home as to whether I dare walk in barefoot or will I meet neighbours in the cul-de-sac?

By now I'm making a habit of getting myself panel-beaten whenever the giving of a training course or the writing of a book takes me to Florida. So on the next trip I hie me to a specialist bunch of foot surgeons there and explain my problem. The surgeon I get is Lebanese and delighted with life, the universe and feet in general. He is so delighted with feet, he even holds on to one of mine, naked (my foot, not him) while we talk, me on an elevated bed/chair, him standing, white-coated. There must be something to this acupuncture notion of connectedness between all the major organs and limbs, since this Lebanese's grasp of my right foot is short-circuiting all my thinking and speaking capabilities.

It's not doing my self-esteem much good, either, which is why I hear myself apologizing when he tells me I have hammertoes. He looks puzzled, and tells me hammertoes are genetic, therefore over them I have no control or influence, never had any control or influence, so why am I apologizing? They run in families, he says. Which explains why my mother has the same kind of twisted feet. I had always assumed she was guilty of her feet, too, because she would never wear "sensible shoes", being given to chic and possessed of the all-time great pair of pins.

Since I was a child, I have been into the prettiest shoes I can find. Fashions like platforms and Doc Martens and the ubiquitous running shoe, I reject without any serious consideration. However, I have always held the belief that my feet would not be so bent and ugly if I had not worn such pretty shoes from such a formative age. Perhaps, in vanity, I have imagined, I squashed all my toes into these awful shapes, so I deserve everything that's coming to me in the toe department.

Thanks to Dr Lebanon's assurance that I am not culpable in this matter, that all I am is a Darwinian failure, I ask him if I am condemned to ongoing misery. Not at all, he says. He can do surgery, he says. But first, let us have a couple of X-rays. He'll be right back. A nurse appears and puts X-ray plates down on a foot-high (appropriately) platform on the floor, over which she positions one of my feet. Having enveloped me in a lead poncho to protect the rest of me from random rays, she retreats out the door, returning about thirty seconds later to do the same thing for the other foot. Dr Lebanon will be right back, she affirms, and I sit/lie there, wondering if all these little X-rays (the implant man will not do anything until he has put me in a chair that does a kind of half turn while the X-ray is on) are going to give me some awful disease. I console myself that I do not smoke and come of a line of long-livers, so maybe that will even up the odds a bit.

Dr Lebanon comes back in and shoves the X-ray films up on a light box on the wall. Curiously enough, what looks bloody awful clothed in flesh, in an X-ray shorn of flesh looks like sophisticated engineering. Dr Lebanon says the main problem on my left foot is the little toe and the toe beside it. Both need straightening out, and the little toe, which has an accretion of bone around the joints that has effectively robbed it of movement, needs bone removed. Ditto the little toe on the other foot, although the toe next to it on that foot does not seem to have marked pathology (his phrase).

It comes as a considerable surprise to me to learn that little toes are supposed to have the same range of movement as other toes. I thought they were meant to huddle helplessly in the shadow of the others, like swaddled babies. Lebanon cannot cope with this at all. He twiddles my right little toe while gesturing at the X-ray.

"But it has all the joints, see?" he says. "Of course it is meant to be used."

I am tempted to point out to him that we all have appendixes, too, but they don't do nothing except get sick and give us pain. Is it his suggestion that because it is there, like Mount Everest (or a miniature organic version of same), it should be expected to work an eight-hour day? That we should all have appendixes and little toes that do not lie about as burdens on the state? No free rides for little toes and appendixes? Instead, I get to the point.

"Exactly what would you do if you were performing this surgery?"

He would make incisions here and here and here, he says, drawing lines down the three toes with his index fingernail. He would go in and he would file down the bump on this toe (the second one). He would go in (on the little toes) and cut away a lot of bone, in order to allow the toe to move. Then he would go in here (about half an inch back from the root of each toe on the upper surface of the foot) and he would weaken the tendon.

He produces a graphic showing the toes being worked by a tendon which, in the case of hammertoes, is usually too tight, like a rubber band; it distorts the shape of the thing it is supposed to assist, pulling the toe into that cramped tightness that results in the hammer shape. If the tendon is weakened by being scraped (shudder, shudder) it will relax a little, allowing the toe to lie down. The cost is about £15,000. Local anaesthetic, and you go home directly after surgery. Someone else driving, obviously.

"How soon can it be done?"

"How soon you want it done?"

"Yesterday."

"How about Friday of this week?"

"What time?"

On Friday, I am prepped with Betadine, which turns my feet bright orange. He then comes in and injects local anaesthetic into them at various points, having warned me that this will be the only painful part of the entire procedure. How right he is. The injections go into five or six sites on each foot, which sites seem to be chosen on the basis that there is bone nearby against which the needle can horrifyingly grind, and which means there is limited space into which the anaesthetic can go, so the injections are long, slow, painful and result in an immediate swelling around the site. Oh joy, oh bliss.

By the time he is finished, I am shaky and shocky. He pats me on the toes and tells me that needs a half an hour to take hold, then buzzes off. For the first time, I note, to the right of the chair/bed in which I am immured with swollen orange feet, a framed notice which says "The speed of your recovery depends on you remembering which of us is the doctor." If I had noticed this on the first consultation, I might have gone somewhere else.

When Dr Lebanon comes back, he comes back covered in assistants, all in surgical greens. One of them rigs up a little thing like a tennis net in front of me, except that in place of the net is an opaque white cloth. I can, if I want, have this removed, she says, but they find that patients prefer not to see what is going on. I acquiesce, but then realize that I can see a colourless reflection of what is going on, down at feet level, in the glass of the notice about remembering who is the doctor. So I have the best of both worlds.

The local anaesthesia may have been hell going in, but Lordy, does it work a treat. I can feel when they hold my heel or one of their hands touches a point far up the instep unreached by the numbing agent, but other than that, I would know they were working on my feet only by the sounds, which are a mixture of the classic "Scalpel, please" instructions from surgeon to assistants and the buzzing of the bone-drill, which sounds like a dentist's drill with big ideas.

"What's the smell of burning?" I ask at one point, hoping the answer would be that it was the inside of the bone drill heating up.

"Your bone," Dr Lebanon says happily.

Hey, I think. Not many people can claim to have smelt their own eyes and their own toes burning. I am kind of a downmarket Joan of Arc. If I had been awake when Dr Brueck did his bit of laser resurfacing, maybe I could have smelled my skin burning, too. Which reminds me that in my younger days, when a fashion for straight hair rendered my naturally wavy hair unacceptable, I would iron my hair before going out at night, so I have smelled my own hair burning too.

The surgery takes nearly an hour and a half. Every time I think he must be finished, Dr Lebanon goes back and has another go. Then he sews them up and down comes the screen ... Time for the lecture, I figure. I am right.

The patient must:

- Keep the feet elevated for at least two days.
- Come back for a check on the second day.
- Come back to have sutures removed a week after surgery.
- Take the painkillers and the antibiotics prescribed. Faithfully – infection in bone is very serious.
- Keep the feet absolutely dry for the first ten days.

After the first ten days, the bulky initial bandages will be removed and replaced with pressure bandages. The patient will be taught how to apply the pressure bandages herself.

Over these bandages, for six months, she will wear shoes, such as walking shoes, which have roomy toe boxes but, despite that, provide a little benign pressure on the bandages which in turn will prevent swelling.

I do not tell him there is no bloody way I am going to live in clumpy shoes for a month, never mind six months. What a surgeon does not know will not hurt him. What a surgeon does know

[186]

will reduce his feelings of responsibility, and I want him feeling responsible, especially after signing one of those ridiculous forms which lays it down that if anything goes wrong, they warned you it was likely to, so why are you whining?

Over the plastering, they put shapeless socks, and over the shapeless socks they put surgical shoes. Surgical shoes are light but horrid. They have stiff styrofoam soles (which explains the lightness) and straps at two points on the foot which are broad and secured by velcro. No matter how fat or narrow your foot, a surgical shoe of roughly the right length can be made to fasten as snugly or as loosely as you want. Surgical shoes are ambidextrous. They do not come in right or left. One gender fits all, and this is arguably why they are so in-your-face repellent.

The nurses fasten me into two surgical shoes fairly snugly and get me onto my feet. While one is grateful, directly after such extensive surgery, to be without pain, it is nonetheless peculiar to have no sensation at all in one's foot from about halfway down. It makes balancing a slight challenge. Also, someone in surgical shoes tends to walk as if they were auditioning to play Frankenstein's monster, since the soles do not bend in the way normal soles of normal shoes do, allowing you to hit the ground heel first and progress to the ball of the foot. Surgical shoes have the same effect on the gait as does wearing flippers, albeit on a slightly smaller scale.

I Frankenstein my way home in a taxi and go to bed. Keeping one's feet elevated, unless one has people to wait on one hand and – Oh, skip it. It is difficult, that's all. In order to stay mobile, I move around the condo on my arse, kidding myself that this will reduce its size and make it firmer.

When it comes to showering, in order to obey orders by keeping the bandage dry, you have a choice. Either you put a plastic bag on each foot, secure it at the ankle with a rubber band and then put another plastic bag outside, secured above the other with a plastic bag, or (my preferred option, since this is one of those long shower boxes) you put a plastic crate at the end of the shower cubicle, get your feet up on that and shower sitting down.

This has disadvantages. You have to narrow the head of the shower so that it sends out a single venomous blade of water, rather than a dispersed spray. You have to gauge the temperature before you get sitting down and then you have to live with whatever you guessed was right. You have to remember to get everything like shampoo, conditioner or loofah down to floor level, as opposed to shelves that are at normal eye level. Plus there's no give in the tiles of a shower, unlike the bottom of a bath, so your bottom protests and stays sore a while.

In the beginning, when the bandaging has to be very thick, my feet will not go into any shoes other than clogs (which have the bowler hat of toe-boxes) or oversized running shoes. I get away with the clogs as long as I can, then begin to economize on the bandaging and make it slightly tighter, on the basis that if I squeeze the toes smaller, even when you take the bandage into account, they will fit into a shoe.

Dr Lebanon did talk about benign pressure, and what could be more benign than tight bandaging? For a couple of days, by the time I go home, my bandaged toes are numb and blue, but other than that we get by, and gradually move from the looser of my shoes to the tighter. Three months after the foot surgery, my right little toe is still about twice the size it used to be, even though it is the same colour as the others. (In the beginning it was an angry red.)

However, there is no hard skin anywhere on it, not a corn within a mile. The skin on it is as soft and smooth as the skin on my fingers.

Moving to the left, the foot where two toes were interfered with: these two are only a third bigger than they would normally be, and the one next to the little toe a thing of beauty, even if a bit overweight. No bumps at the joints. No bumps anywhere. It flows straight from the instep to the toenail in one elegant line and the only thing that bothers me is why I didn't have the whole lot of my toes done to match it. The reason I did not have this done, of course, was that I was starting from a motivation of pain, not of beauty. I wanted the chronic corn formation on those two toes, occasioned by the bony lumps under the skin, halted before the pain drove me up a tree.

Six months later there is no pain of any kind, no matter what choice of shoes I make in the morning. Not only is there no pain, but all my toes have smooth skin and not the smallest embryonic corn. There was no need to have other toes done because corns never formed on them anyway.

(However, they are still ugly, the toes that are plastic-surgery virgins, and I now imagine that if I had them all interfered with to take away the bumps, de-hammer the hammers, and flatten them all out in a row of sardine-like neatness, my feet would be so visually improved that people would pay money just to see them. Or at least I might pose for a photograph in jeans with no shoes on. For *People* magazine. They're very into bare feet at *People*.)

Being realistic about this (which, in the context of this book, I appreciate may not sound like the kind of approach usually taken by me), I know I do not need my other toes flattened out, but I do make a point of telling Tom that, although it would make them much more attractive, I will be forbearing and not go for the extra surgery I am sure Dr Lebanon would undertake at the drop of a scalpel. Tom is unimpressed by this. I get shirty with Tom and ask why he is unimpressed, which is foolish of me.

"You are not going for the extra foot surgery," Tom says, "because first of all you wouldn't have the courage to go through that local anaesthetic again. You really hated it."

"And second of all?"

"Second of all, you're working up to something else, probably on your face, and while you will have no compunction about a second mortgage in order to achieve that, a third mortgage would be required to do the rest of your toes as well, so seven little piggies are going to have to stay at home."

He's right. I'll tell you in the next chapter about the bit of facial surgery he spotted me working up to. In the meantime, let's sign off on the feet. Am I glad I did it? Absolutely – the benefit to my face alone is visible. I no longer (even though there is still residual healing pain from deep in the bones) have a face wizened with corn-pain at the end of every day. My shoe size went down one. Always a rival to Imelda Marcos, I now find myself window-shopping for shoes, and even dropping in at the web site featuring the tallest heels (steel-rod reinforced) in the world, in ordinary (for me) and huge sizes (for transvestites, probably). It's at www. sexyshoe.com, if you want a snoop.

COST: £1,290 and immobility for a few weeks
VERDICT: 10 out of 10

11

Scarless endoscopic brow-lift

Some advertising genius, somewhere, dreamed up the slogan, "You can't eat just one" for something like potato crisps.

Same thing applies to cosmetic surgery. You can't stop at one procedure. I found I couldn't, anyway.

Yes, it was delightful to get up in the morning, stumble into the bathroom and, leaving the shower, find a smooth-cheeked unwattly face looking back at me from the mirror. Yes, it was pleasant to buy close-fitting knit skirts, knowing that one's stomach would stay flat beneath the knit, courtesy of liposuction. Yes, it was great to be able to put on long-wearing make-up at dawn and not have to screw it up by taking out one's contact lenses when, after eight hours, they signalled that they'd had enough.

But there were areas still falling short of a satisfactory mark. One was my forehead, which looked as if someone had taken a barbeque fork and scraped it laterally, leaving me with three and a half broad-spaced, deep, deep lines. So deep were they that whenever I got sunburned, if I pushed at my hairline, the lines showed up white against the tan of the rest of my forehead.

Having done its work with the barbeque fork, time/gravity and dissipation had then taken an ordinary fork and scored me up and down between the brows, leaving furrows so deep, I was essentially a frown waiting to happen. Simple personal observation and its related desire to Get Something Done About what I was seeing in the mirror were reinforced by another habit of the plastic-surgery addict: reading up about the latest developments. In doing such reading, I learned that gravity pulls down your eyebrows. Your forehead skin has enough "give" in it to allow it to develop wrinkles and still stretch enough to lower your eyebrows into the next parish.

Lowered eyebrows contribute to a depressed look sometimes justified by advancing age and time. Try lifting your own forehead so the eyebrows come up and you will see that the minute the brows rise, the spirits seem to rise with them. What I had not realized is that gravity does not stop at the brows. No way. Gravity takes a look at the nose and says, "Whee, let's swing offa the end of this," which Gravity then does, lengthening the nose and turning it down. The result is that in one's forties and fifties, one has a longer nose than in one's teens and twenties, and the length is exacerbated by droop.

Reflecting on this, I was reminded of the Old Witch syndrome first raised in connection with bone loss subsequent to tooth loss. Bone loss made your face cave in, go concave and point your chin upwards. Gravity doing a swing-swong off the end of your nose pointed the schnozzle downwards, so, on a bad day, chin and nose might meet in front of your mouth.

The first priority, clearly, was to get the upper-jaw implant saga finished. More than five years after the whole thing started, I was still attending the dental surgeon who had first introduced my jawbone to titanium. We were ostentatiously not blaming each other for the drawn-out duration of the saga, although he did say reproachfully, when my two natural front teeth began to wobble in a hopeless kind of way and he had to remove them, that this forced him back to the drawing board; but because some of the posts were already in place, he could not do the more modern procedures developed since the two of us had started down the implant path.

Finally, the technician presented his *magnum opus*, an opalescent beauty: a set of upper teeth in porcelain to be screwed in, cemented down and forgotten about. Well, not quite forgotten about. Dental hygiene is, if anything, more important for someone with implants than for someone with natural teeth, and so when I finally departed his surgery, beaming at the world through astonishingly white teeth, I took with me all sorts of funny toothbrushes and systems for getting into the tiny spaces between teeth and gums.

The effort would be worth it. To be able to laugh out loud without laying a concealing hand over one's open mouth is such a freedom. To bite into an apple unselfconsciously is such a joy. To chew the toughest steak would be easy. Here's the truth. I now own only four teeth of my own. But I have no dentures. No living out of a glass. No coming off a flight and not being able to brush one's teeth because of the need to take out a bridge and the impossibility of so doing when there are other people in the airport restroom.

Very few people need to have a complete mouthful of implants, so the cost should not put anybody off looking at implant possibilities. They have got cheaper during the time I was going through the system. Cheaper – and faster. My own dental implant expert now does what he calls same-day teeth. Implants by teatime. There are also more options. For example, someone who already has false lower teeth and doesn't want to embark on full implants can now have a couple of posts inserted to act almost as anchor tenants, holding a denture rock-solid.

"It's a huge advantage to someone who has a lower plate that shifts all the time," my dental surgeon pointed out. "And it costs less than £2,500."

VERDICT, DENTAL IMPLANTS TOP AND BOTTOM: 9 out of 10 (the minus 1 is just because it took so long)

Because of the implants, my face is going to be less inclined to go in a concave banana curve. But dental implants will not solve the problem of the overhanging nose.

A look back at the photograph album can be a depressing experience. I tried it. There it was, in my teens, this attractive, optimistic, slightly upward-looking nose. Short and sweet. Beautifully fitted into the face. Not a seam showing.

Compare the old photographs with the mirror reflection of today, and the contrast is not striking, but notable. So here I am, with the lower part of my face in great shape but being invaded from above by brows and a nose with territorial ambitions. This, on its own, would be a minor irritant. Combined with the deepening furrows on my forehead, though, it moved, if not into the category of Problem To Be Instantly Fixed, at least in to the category of Problem To Be Researched.

So I look into the brow-lift issue. Brow-lifts have traditionally taken the form of what Tom would disapprovingly call Plastic Surgical Mutilation. In other words, the surgeon cuts into the scalp starting at the ears and goes across, Alice-band fashion, an inch down behind the hairline, to the other ear. The surgeon then loosens the skin down to the eyebrows, hauls the whole lot of it up, cuts off the spare and sutures the remainder together behind the hairline.

A tad crude, I hear you say. Regardless of the crudity, the fact is that after a brow-lift, the patient has a taut, smoothed-out brow, uplifted eyebrows and a generally alert, rested and optimistic expression. The procedure can be done under general anaesthetic or a combination of what several of the surgeons have taken to calling "twilight sleep" combined with some local anaesthesia. Properly done, the effects last from six to ten years, with one small disadvantage of transient hair loss sometimes occurring around where the incision was. The scars are, of course, hidden within the hair.

I am giving this serious consideration when I hear about the "Scarless endoscopic brow-lift". I read up a little about it, and on a business trip to Florida find a free seminar being given by a surgeon alleged to be one of the pioneers of this new procedure, and go along.

This seminar is on a different scale from the one I attended before I got into this face-lift, brow-lift jag. It is held in a concert hall. I and about two hundred other people scatter ourselves throughout an auditorium capable of holding three times as many.

There are drinks (including alcoholic, even though it is a lunchtime seminar) and snacks. Glossy literature on every chair, which makes much use of visual references to classical statues. I always find this questionable as a promotional tool for plastic surgeons, since the statutes they use tend, by the nature of ancient statues, to have vital bits missing, and I should have thought some of the patients or potential patients might make a negative subliminal connection. They never seem to do so, though.

When a sufficient number are gathered together, the surgeon appears on the stage beside a huge screen and begins his talk, which starts, as all these talks seem to do, from the wrong place, which is, "How you should pick me and only me as your cosmetic surgeon of choice because the world out there is full of guys masquerading to be as good as me, but some of them are plumbers in disguise". It is never cast in quite such blatant terms, but you get my drift.

Because he starts in the wrong place, I stop paying attention to content and, by way of distraction to myself, chronicle the man's presentation flaws, which are many. He seems to have a partly corrected stammer, which produces pregnant pauses at unpredictable moments throughout the talk, and a conviction that the essential truth of what he is saying is to be found deep in his right-hand trouser pocket. He delves deeply and anxiously into this directly after most of his pregnant pauses. When the sequence is established, it has a pleasing rhythm to it.

Having warned us not to talk to strangers in the cosmetic surgery business, he moves on to rubbish what almost everybody else in that business is still (condemning sigh, pregnant pause, delve in pocket) doing: the traditional brow-lift. He goes through the atrocities of the brow-lift with such muted horror, he leaves everyone in the audience wondering how any sane person, no matter how vain and withered, ever subjected themselves to such defacement.

Then he announces that he is going to show us a videotape of this revolutionary new procedure he has perfected, to do away with all the nasties associated with the older procedure. This videotape turns out to be the most singular, not to say queer, visual aid adduced thus far in my quest to understand and profit from plastic surgery. It is shot from behind the surgeon while he operates, and so we can see nothing of the procedure. Lest you think I speak metaphorically, let me tell you that this is the straight-up truth. We get to view the machine out of which the endoscope comes. We get to see, in a medium close-up of somewhat defective focus clarity, an endoscope. We get to see the patient beforehand. But the surgery? Nothing.

Having thus brought our ignorance to a higher level, Dr Pregnant Pause explains that he shoves the endoscope in at the top of the head, threads it down through the face, hooks on to a muscle, hauls the muscle back up to where it should have been had not gravity done its awful deeds, and sticks it in its new place. He does this a number of times throughout the face, hauling up the key muscles, including those around the mouth that give the droopy look when they sag.

If the face on which he is operating has gone lopsided or was (as he puts it) asymmetrical to begin with to an unpleasing extent, he yanks up the muscles on one side of the face more than on the other side. This, he claims, gives a much more subtle, lasting and real look than the old traditional brow- and face-lifts. He shows us examples, pointing out that whereas a regular face-lift on Face A would pull back the spare skin, it would still leave the person with a bunch of fallen muscle at the jaw line, whereas with the endoscopic face-lift, the roundness is restored to the cheeks as the muscles which should be located there are brought back up. This is not counting the effect of adding a personal fat pad, which rounds out the parts of the face getting thin with age even more.

Fat taken from another part of the body sounds like good budgeting to me, especially when he says that his experience is that the imported fat does not tend to migrate away from the area where it's put. He tells it to sit and stay and it sits and stays.

Now is where the thing gets icky, if you come from the other side of the Atlantic. He shows us pictures of a woman in her late thirties or early forties. (He tells us her precise age, but I forget.) The Before pictures show her looking well into her forties and depressed with it. Her face is fat, but fat in a saggy way. Then he puts up the After pictures, which show her looking as if she is in her late thirties and healthy with it. Never mind healthy, is she happy? Is she what! She glows in the After pictures. The face is still fat, but much more pleasing, because the fat has moved up to pull her face back to a pleasing ovoid (his term; "egg-shaped" to you).

Reacting delightedly to positive audience reaction, Dr Pause shares with us that this patient is his wife. I am stunned by the notion of him operating on someone in his family, I thought the Hippocratic oath or something like that prevented a surgeon from going to work on those close to him. Just as remarkable, to me, is that his wife would have allowed him to use her as an advertisement. He seems to feel – and audience reaction reinforces the impression – that it is the ultimate romantic gesture to stick an endoscope in the top of your wife's head to drag up the infrastructure of her face and leave it hanging on higher hooks.

Going into even more close-up shots of his wife, he points out that, although he did not touch the tip of her nose with a scalpel nor remove any part of it, still, on the second pictures, her nose appears shorter and more optimistic. Perky, even, he suggests after a pause and a delve into his pocket.

"Perky, ho ho, isn't he sweet?" goes the audience.

This perkiness apparently results from the fact that an endoscopic brow-lift, in lugging upward the muscles of the forehead, corrects the gravity distorting the length of the nose, because the upwardly mobile muscles give an uplift to the muscles supporting it.

He shows another video, this time genuinely helpful to the understanding of the process, of the laser resurfacing process in action, and then turns to nose-jobs.

There is a technical term for them which I can neither spell nor pronounce, but this surgeon never uses anything but that technical term. He obviously has an objection to the phrase "nose-job". This time his pictorial examples are two young men with an over-supply of nose. That's in the Before shots. In the After shots, the same two young lads are beaming. (Fundamental rule of all After shots shown by plastic surgeons: patient must beam, even if straightforward comparison with Before shots would clearly be easier if the patient wore the same expression in each.)

The lecturer allows us to savour the radical difference made to the appearance of the now charming youngsters and then admits that they are his sons. The eldest, he tells us, asked for a nose-job (using the technical term, no doubt) as a birthday present when he was about to turn sixteen. The result was so satisfactory that the younger son asked for precisely the same birthday gift at the same age. This seminar seems to be turning into Family Demonstration Hour, and a little nasty thought, one of those sprouting miniature horns and a tail, strikes. Is he using family in pictures because he has not done much work on paying customers?

He accidentally answers this sneaky question. Accidentally and over the long haul, because he first of all shows us a bundle of pictures of improvements he has wrought on mostly female members of his staff. He has taken an endoscope to so many of them, one cannot help but wonder if it's one of the perks of signing on to work for him. Brow-lifts, face-lifts, symmetry work, lasers – you name it, he has done it to one of his staff.

Their photographs are up there on the big screen to validate every one of the procedures, and at the end of every example, he invites a human-scale smiling woman onto the stage beneath her oversized image to beam at us and take a round of applause which in my view is completely unjustified. If they had taken an endoscope to themselves, maybe a round of applause would have been earned, but they were just the victims.

He seems to have no male staff. Lucky, I think, that he had sons to operate on, or his demo models would have been exclusively female.

He finishes and requests questions. Very few get asked, although I do put my hand up and enquire why the hell he showed us a video of the procedure which leaves us as pig-ignorant of what the procedure is really like as we were before he played it. He nods as if he wanted to be asked this query, explaining that he finds when people get to see what actually happens, they faint a lot, so it seemed better just to give us a flavour, you know? The audience knows. The audience laughs merrily at their own attributed delicacy of response and thinks he is only the bee's knees for sizing them up so well. I would go after him, except I am distracted by noticing that when he is answering questions, he has neither pregnant pauses nor delvings into pockets.

I go for a computer-assisted discussion with him a couple of days later. They take me into a little white-walled room where a digital camera is sitting on a tripod, and take full frontal and both profile photographs of me before taking the film (or disc) plus me into a room with a computer which has an extra large screen on it. They feed the disc into the computer and I pop up on screen, looking startled, also very wrinkly as to the forehead.

"That's you," sparkles the assistant, who looks familiar. She turns out to be Mrs Pause, recently made more ovoid by his skilled hands. She invites me to tell her what I want achieved for me. Smooth forehead, I say. She electronically erases my forehead wrinkles. Eyebrows up just short of astounded, I say. I don't mind looking a bit surprised, but not so's I resemble a spectator at the Second Coming.

Up come the eyebrows. Nose up, I say, like a submarine pilot. Nose comes up. That little jowly bit gone, I say, forgetting I am supposedly planning only a forehead-lift, and the little jowly bit goes. Corners of mouth undrooped, I say, and the corners of my mouth come up to just this side of quirky. I look at the image on the screen. It is still me, but me as I fancy I look after a good rest and some positive news.

Go for it, I tell Ms Ovoid. Tell me how much it will set me back. She does a lot of sums and tells me that between one thing and another, I am looking at £10,000. Not that she should be telling me this, she adds, visibly unnerved by my getting so quickly to the point. Presumably most patients to and fro a little before they agree to have foreign bodies on wires inserted in their faces and remote-controlled.

At this point, Dr Pregnant Pause arrives, looks at the original of the video shots, looks at the improved version, agrees it is possible, says it will cost even slightly less than Ms Ovoid has guesstimated, and says he'll throw in a little laser resurfacing to the corners of the mouth and fat pads to the cheeks for the same price, if I'd like.

I baulk, for no good reason, at the fat pads but go along with the lasering. How soon can they do it? They start talking eight weeks away and I indicate that I have this obsessive-compulsive problem that once I have decided to do something like this, I need to do it yesterday or everybody's life within a ten-mile radius is not worth living.

Ms Ovoid says doubtfully that they had a cancellation for two days hence, but I wouldn't want that. Yes I would, I say. But they couldn't do the blood work in the time, she says. Of course you could, I reassure her, and Dr Pause laughs and says he'll see me in theatre.

Two days later. Dawn. Earlier than dawn, if we're to be accurate. Consultation with surgeon. Him in greens, me in a robe. Location: day-surgery centre. My belongings are already sealed in a bag somewhere else. I have little socks on my feet. All of which robs me of authority and presence. He checks through the results of the blood work, weighs me without explanation, puts indelible pen marks on my face and goes away.

A nurse anaesthetist gets me on to a trolley and puts in an I/V. Effortlessly. Painlessly. Beautifully. I ask her some question and never register the answer because what is flowing through the I/V knocks me cold.

The following morning I get out of bed without difficulty, and examine myself. I look like a blowfish. My face is not only swollen, but angry red around the mouth. My mouth must not like a laser getting so close to it, and so my lips have swollen up. Even as a blowfish, my smooth forehead pleases me, but does not deceive me. I've been here before. I know that as the swelling goes down, some of the wrinkling comes back. Some, not all. Not by any means all.

I do the post-operative visit, at which I discover that all the spare forehead skin is stapled in place on the top of my head. I have an astonishing ridge of piled-up skin, with about 408 strong metal staples pinning it to my brain. (I exaggerate, but only by a dozen or two.) High-tech hygienic version of Marlene Dietrich's hairpin, I think. It is like wearing a cast-iron Alice band. Not surprisingly, it gives me a fairly constant headache.

Which reminds me – this is not the only headache provoked by plastic surgery. In the direct aftermath of the face-lift, I had a headache I thought I might die from, and when, on a post-operative visit, the surgeon paid no attention to it, I told him this was a Richter-scale 9 headache.

"Caffeine withdrawal," he said unsympathetically. "Often happens to our patients. Give up coffee permanently and then you will never again have that problem as a result of having to stay off coffee for twelve hours before a general anaesthetic."

I ignored him, of course. Coffee is one of the essentials of living.

Before the endoscope went to work on me, I had resolved to make some notes – almost keep a diary – about the recovery. What follows is taken from that diary.

It's now two weeks since Dr Pause went to work on me. I am fresh out of the shower, notebook PC on terry-clothed lap, ready to do an inventory.

Starting at the top.

I think at this stage I have washed the remaining bits of dried blood out of my hair. Still have the cast-iron Alice band running from temple to temple. Slightly raised up. It's as if the surgeon mixed plaster of Paris plus anaesthetic into a paste and inserted it under the skin in a line two inches broad, starting about an inch back from my hairline. Quite a pleasant sensation. Makes one's scalp more interesting than it usually is.

I could do the Marlene Dietrich hairpin routine at the moment, no bother, because there's no feeling in the Alice band bit of my scalp. Of course, now I don't need to do it ...

Checking over my face with the points of my fingernails, I find the middle bit of my forehead has feeling, but not too much of it. The lasered bit is now a subdued, not to say tired, red, and has no more sensitivity than unlasered skin. From my temples to below my cheekbones is numb. There's a random bit of numbness, too, on the right side of my upper lip. The kind of last-ditch numbness you get three hours after the dentist finished a root-canal on you.

Good news about the endoscopic attack is that my forehead

has prolapsed just enough to make me look natural. I no longer have that resemblance to an stunned blowfish. My right cheek-bone feels padded, but it doesn't look as if someone hid half a banana under the eye. Although that side still swells in the morning, it no longer looks as if Tom put me to sleep by hitting me with a two-by-four. Now it looks like he put me to sleep with a soft sock full of damp sand.

Worryingly, my eyesight has disimproved. I had kind of noticed this over the past week, but last night became sure of it, because they were running the story of Bill Clinton's admission that he did something inappropriate to Monica Lewinsky, and part of the report had his wife, last January, in a big close-up, saying something he contradicted today. I realized, watching, that I couldn't make out any of the details of Hillary's face, and even squinting didn't pull her features into focus. Question: Is this because the laser did something to my eyes or is it that pulling one side of one's face up puts one eye at a different angle or is the back of the eye subject to some of the swelling on that side? I'm curious, rather than bothered ...

It took six weeks for my eyesight to get back to improved normal, but get back it did. My face stopped swelling at night, my cheek-bone went back to what a cheekbone should be, and I went back to work (after three weeks' "summer holidays") to glad cries of how good the holiday must have been because I looked so marvellous.

Verdict on scarless endoscopic brow-lift?

The best.

COST: £5,700 and a week looking peculiar
VERDICT: 11 out of 10

It does leave you with a slightly bumpy scalp, but unless you're planning to shave your head, you're not likely to care.

12

Paralysing my forehead

Because I was so enthusiastic about my smoothed-out forehead, I was eager to ensure that it stayed that way. Which turned me into a sitting duck for an ad in a Florida paper inviting people to attend a seminar about Botox and its effects on wrinkles. I have heard just enough about Botox to be interested and to go along. The seminar is in an eye clinic, the reason being that the use of Botox started with ophthalmic surgeons.

The ophthalmic surgeon delivering the talk is so bouncy, you want to put him in diving boots to keep him in the one spot. He is enthusiastic about hydroxy acids, he is thrilled about exfoliation, and when it comes to stimulating the formation of collagen in the dermis (by regular exfoliation) he is damn nearly orgasmic, particularly about what he calls "the lunch-hour peel".

Then he gets down to the wrinkle business, spending about ten minutes defining wrinkles as either dynamic or static. This distinction is of no value whatever. The only wrinkles any of us want to know about are the kind we get when we raise our eyebrows or smile. Expression wrinkles. Anyway, having made this esoteric distinction between wrinkles, he then admits that most start as dynamic wrinkles and gradually become static wrinkles.

That means that after years and years of raising the average eyebrow, you have wrinkles that, even when you relax, will still be visible. The oftener you repeat an expression, the deeper the wrinkle becomes.

Having established that we all know what he's talking about when he talks wrinkles, he moves on to talk Botox. Back to definitions. This, we are exalted to hear, is a purified neurotoxin.

Don't get euphemistic with me, Buddy, I think. This is a close relative of *clostridium botulinim*, a bacterium in canned foods that haven't been canned properly. Eat enough of it in innocence, it'll kill you.

"When that neurotoxin is liberated into your system, it can paralyse muscles," the Botox man admits. "The most common one is the diaphragm, which you use for breathing, and that's what you often hear about in these bad cases of botulism: patients who have to be put on a respirator if the diaphragm isn't working."

His small audience looks depressed. He senses this, and offers the good side of the story.

"Like many things nowadays," he announces, "what can be a devastating problem in high doses can be a very beneficial agent in smaller doses and that's what's happened with Botox. It blocks the transmission between the nerve and the muscle. By blocking the transmission, we can temporarily weaken the muscle that we inject this agent into. Allergan Pharmaceutical, who make this toxin, precipitate it out in very small amounts for use to weaken muscle. This was not developed for cosmetic use; it was developed for patients who had a functional problem, say, for example, patients who couldn't keep their eyes open.

"It's used for that and for other movement disorders. But in the course of treating, somebody made the observation that if you weaken a muscle, sometimes you reduce a wrinkle associated with it, and so they began to play around with it for cosmetic use."

He then explains that the way they administer the stuff is that, first, they put local anaesthetic cream on the areas planned for injection and leave them for twenty minutes to thirty minutes to get the skin to numb.

"The injections are given with tuberculin syringe needles, which are very very small needles, thirty-gauge needles, and we're putting it just under the skin," he adds. "We don't need to go deep into the muscle, because once it gets into the skin, it'll diffuse into the muscle on its own gradually over the course of one or two days. The peak effect is after two weeks and, as the body breaks down the toxin, the effect wears off, after maybe three months to six months or so."

He admits that there are occasional side-effects. Botox, on occasion, drifts from the brow into the eyelid, creating a droopy lid or – if it gets into one of the muscles around the eye – double vision, if injected too deeply. None of his illustrations show anything of that nature. His illustrations show people shot full of Botox, their wrinkles at rest. When he has finished showing them to us, he indicates that he will take questions now on any aspect of what he has covered. He gets taken up on this offer, and I record what follows on my dictaphone. Catching, I hope, the truth, and the whole truth. Plus a couple of very individual pronunciations.

[209]

Q. How long have you been using Botox?

A. Since my second year of residency, which was back in 1988. Back then, of course, we weren't doing it for cosmetic reasons, but for where patients had heavy facial spasm or blepharospasm: squeezing around the eyes. I started using it for seven or eight years before I started using it cosmetically. It's a lot more difficult with these patients with squeezing problems, because you have to use much higher doses and you have to be in areas where there's the potential for more problems. Cosmetically, it's not that difficult.

Q. How many people have you treated with Botox?

A. I wouldn't know how many injections I've done, but it's in the several hundreds, maybe even a thousand.

Q. Have you ever had any drift?

A. Drift? Botox – it depends. You know, if you inject too deep or too much, you prolly could have a drift, but I use very small doses and inject just under the skin, so I really haven't had a drift. You know, in some of the blepharospasm patients where we're giving higher doses, if you go down below the cheeks in here, you could have some going to the lower face and that might create some problems.

Q. Is this a lunch-hour procedure?

A. (*Laughs*) Yes it is. It really only takes – the longest part is to have the cream on to numb it up, but it prolly takes me sixty seconds or something like that to do the injections and that's if you're having everything. We divided it into three areas, and not everyone wants all that done. I charge by the aesthetic area. So if you want the eyes, it's $200, if you want the forehead, it's $200, if you want the frown, it's $300. The reason it's expensive is that the agent itself costs $350 a bottle. There's only one company making it. It was an orphan drug. When they developed it, they didn't think there was going to be much application for it. Now it's selling like crazy because people are using it for cosmetic reasons and they're making money on it, but because they had a lot of cost in developing this and they had to build a whole plant to make this stuff, and so they're millions and millions of dollars in deficit and they need to recoup some of that money, so they need to charge $350 a bottle.

Q. Do you think this is better than collagen?

A. It's very different. Collagen was filling in volume where there's a crease, smoothing that crease out. If you have a very big crease and you inject collagen into the skin, that'll make the skin plump and relieve the crease out of the skin. The problem with it is that one, it's very technique-dependent; if you can't give it in the right place, it doesn't work at all. Two is that all the collagen disappears in a couple of weeks.

Most people who use collagen use it because they want to look good for one night. (*Stir of disbelief.*) Some people, that's OK, I guess. But it's not long-lasting at all. With Botox, you're not effecting any change in the skin itself, you're just weakening the muscle beneath the skin, underneath the wrinkle, so it's much more effective in the sense that a very small amount paralyses the muscle to the point that the skin relaxes and the wrinkle disappears, albeit temporarily, but we're talking months rather than days to weeks, so yeah, I think it's preferable. I've never understood wanting to treat crow's feet with collagen, that would be so tedious and so difficult. And still, when you smile, you're gonna crease the skin ...

Before he is finished, I go out to the front desk and ask if I can have Botox injections that afternoon. They scurry around and say that if I can wait about thirty minutes, they can facilitate me.

I am ushered into a traditional ophthalmic office, eye-test card on the wall and all, to have the pre-injection numbing agent dabbed on to me with a Q-tip, and left to marinade for half an hour. After that time, the man who has been giving the seminar arrives in a white coat. He takes some details, agrees that the brow-lift can be best maintained if the forehead is not allowed to be expressive and to recreate the lines removed by the endoscope, and goes to work.

It is uncomfortable, rather than painful. Because one's skull bone is so near the surface on the forehead, there is the sensation that the needle is crunching against it. For a couple of seconds on every stab, there is pain. Sixteen stabs in all. I go away, and after two days, have a pretty immobile forehead and virtually no capacity to frown.

Not only does this help preserve my wrinkle-less state, but it has a strangely beneficent side-effect: when I want to frown and find my own forehead solidly resisting me, it forces me to examine the mood I'm in. Strange to say it, but an immobilized frown-space can greatly improve one's personality. One tries to live up to the benign exterior established by plastic surgery and killer toxins.

One of the things I do for a living is train newsreaders and other performers for television. They frequently have a problem that – unbeknownst to themselves – they raise their eyebrows in time with every upward inflection. This has two disadvantages. It is very distracting to viewers. That's the short-term disadvantage. Longer term, of course, the performers develop deep forehead furrows, making them look much older and much more worried than they are. As part of working with me, they have to retrain their facial muscles so that they stop the brow-raising. It is incredibly difficult, because the habit is an involuntary one. Since I discovered Botox, I have simply told them to short-circuit the retraining and get the muscles paralysed. If they want to skill-build, let them skill-build in diction and let the botulism bug take care of the eyebrow department.

Since that first set of injections, I have had Botox injected four times into my own face. The suggestion that it lasts six months I have not found to be borne out in fact, and indeed a couple of Botox-supplying doctors have confirmed that, for many people, three months is the duration of its effectiveness. That is not to say that at the end of twelve weeks, one's brow starts leaping about and forming wrinkles as fast as it can. I just mean that when twelve weeks have passed, the beginnings of instinctive movement are beginning to come back.

Some of the doctors who have injected me with this stuff do not put on numbing cream beforehand. This is an advantage. Numbing cream or no numbing cream, when a needle goes into your forehead and crunches against your skull, there is going to be brief pain, and in my view, hanging about waiting for a cream to take effect, knowing that the effect it has is going to be minimal is a waste of time. I would rather have the procedure be a little more painful and a lot more fast.

Because they inject perhaps twelve different sites on the forehead and below the eyes (to prevent crows' feet) and because it takes a couple of hours for the Botox to fully disperse from the original injection site, having had a Botox session, you need to go home fairly directly. Your face has the appearance of having been painfully stung by mosquitoes. However, a day later, paralysis kicks in and your forehead boasts neither a bite-hill nor a forehead furrow. All this for a cost ranging between £250 and £650. (I cannot find out why some charge less than half what other medics charge for precisely the same service.)

COST: £400 and an afternoon off work, because the needle-sticks are visible, like recent bee-stings
VERDICT: 10 out of 10

That 10 is predicated on a previous brow-lift. I don't believe Botox injections, even over a long and continuous period of time, would do away with the kind of lines I had, pre-lift. Having got rid of them, though, Botox plays a blinder when it comes to keeping them from coming back.

It's now possible to get Botox from your friendly local GP at about fifty quid a go, and you need to do it about every three months.

13

Wait for next year's thrilling instalment

Here's a prediction for you.

In the first ten years of this new century, plastic surgery for cosmetic purposes will become as fashionable as running, gym-going and visits to health farms were in the nineties. More cost perhaps. But less effort. Less time. More tangible, palpable, visible results.

The time factor matters. Particularly for women, who are under most pressure, as far as appearance goes, anyway. Women work on average ninety hours a week between career and home, whatever home is. Getting their face fixed while they're on their summer holidays may not sound as much fun as sand, sea and sex, but the outcome, in terms of looks, confidence and restedness, is a hell of a lot better.

They will save up for surgery, take out a second mortgage, decide on a boob-pullup rather than putting hardwood floors into the drawing-room – because they have been brought up to instant, rather than deferred, gratification. Their mothers bought jars of cream and convinced themselves that subtle improvements resulted over time. They want visible improvements, right now. They no longer believe the lies.

It sounds like a contradiction in terms, but until I got into plastic surgery, I lived a lie. Several lies.

The lie of "cleanse, tone and moisturize in order to have beautiful skin throughout life".

The lie that running and other exercises would make me live forever and be forever young. (I believed that until it dawned on me that runners after a year or so get haggard and skinny, and a surprising number drop dead. In the living-forever stakes, picking your parents is the best option, and I come from a line of long livers, so the hell with running.)

The biggest lie I bought was the feminist promise that we would create a world where a woman's talent, competence, insight and special qualities would be valued above her appearance. My arse. The blondes are still draped over the bonnets of new cars and the babes in suits get promoted over the bright battleaxes every time.

At first (as in, right now) people like me will have their faces lifted, sanded, fat-sucked and strategically fat-padded and they will not let on that they have done it. (In which practice they follow generations of actresses explaining away their maintained beauty by claiming a healthy lifestyle, with lots of chicken, fish and vegetables. Yeah, right.)

They will not let on that they have done it, for a number of reasons.

First of all, because they don't need the instant personal trivialization that happens when people know about a face-lift. For some reason, public perception removes the brain of the person who had the "lift". Not just the brain, but the talent, reputation and position. That person is defined from then by the face-lift: witness Julie Christie.

Anybody want to take bets on whether a journalist will ever interview Julie Christie again without majoring on the face-lift? Unless, of course, ignoring the face-lift is a pre-condition of getting the interview, in which case the hack will express his/her integrity by majoring on it in the feature subsequently written.

Another reason people will not admit to having had this kind of surgery is that they do not need the judgemental glances. The glances that say: "You had a face-lift? Laser resurfacing? Didn't make you beautiful, did it? Wasn't worth it, was it?" People meeting you don't compare you with what you would have looked like, at this age, without surgery. They compare you to their personally created ideal, and you always fall short, thereby facilitating the judgement that the surgery was an egregious waste of money.

At a time when traditional virtues have fallen away, people define themselves as virtuous by the things they do not do – hence the ones who believe themselves to be signally authentic and demonstrably profound because they would never have plastic surgery. The ones who see character in creases, wisdom in wizenedness. The ones who say jocosely, with the apparent conviction that they are the first to say it, "Hey, I wouldn't get rid of these wrinkles. I *earned* these wrinkles!"

Then they usually go on to suggest that face-lifts are a snare and a delusion because if you look at the hands of someone who has had a face-lift, their true age shows through in their hands.

But if authenticity truly lies in revealing the "true age", why do people take such malicious delight in outing it?

Not that it's just age-related, any more. Many plastic surgery providers have noted a considerable shift, within the past two or three years, from older, wealthier patients to younger patients with less money. One surgeon ran his finger down a list of patients booked for surgery with him the following week and told me 60 per cent of them were under thirty-five; three of them were nurses, one was a teacher, two were secretaries.

One of the reasons for the drop in age must be the drop in price. Most of the procedures listed in this book have become cheaper since I had them, even though as little as two years has elapsed in some cases. It's possible, now, for example, to get LASIK work done in the US for $450 per eye. Not only are prices dropping but – to make face-lifts and boob-jobs more accessible to non-millionaires – some American providers are now doing it on the instalment system. In front of me is a newspaper ad which goes like this:

Breast Augmentation	$4,200 / $118 month
Liposuction	$2,200 / $75 month
Upper Eyelid-Lift	$2,000 / $70 month
Lip Enhancement	$1,000 / $20 month

This pattern fits into an emerging niche holiday market: the plastic-surgery trip. Irish people already head for Florida for sun, sea, tennis and quiet surgical interventions. South Africa is competing very strongly for the same business, with Web sites offering safari/surgery holidays at competitive rates.

As long as I have to work with people, I will invest in mutilating methods to prevent them dismissing me because I am an ageing woman. (As soon as I no longer have to work with people, I may abandon all this and settle into a scarred and saggy senility.) I will do this, not because I believe in the importance of looks, but because I believe in the importance of what I have to offer, other than looks, and I am realistic enough to know that what I have to offer will be progressively devalued because of the natural deterioration in my looks if I don't intervene.

How sad? That people judge you on your looks and make a negative judgement because those looks can reveal advancing years? Very.

Sad that I would cater for that reality by having mutilating surgery? No. Expensive, maybe. Sad, no.

Some day, people may stop judging the book by the cover. I don't know about you, but even though I'm an optimist, I'm not holding my breath. Changing the attitudes and behaviours of large numbers of people takes time. Ask an African-American. Or a gay person. It could take a century or two to change Western cultures so that age regains the perceived value it had in the past. That is assuming such change is possible. Given the reversal past square one which happened after the first fine careless rapture of women's liberation, I, personally, doubt it, but go ahead, Grey Panthers, prove me wrong. *Please* prove me wrong.

Even if it was agreed by nations, by ad agencies and by media in general that ageing and its physical manifestations are good and admirable things, and even if campaigns were relentlessly run to convince the general public that this was the case, it would take a century or two to reach any kind of critical mass.

My generation – the forty-somethings – do not have a century or two at their disposal.

We'll make do with cosmetic surgery.

Even enjoy it.

Perhaps get addicted to it ...